# WEAVE *with* WORDS

# WEAVE *with* WORDS

## USING INLAY *to* CREATE TEXT *in* WOVEN CLOTH

*Scott Norris*

SCHIFFER CRAFT
4880 Lower Valley Road • Atglen, PA 19310

**Other Schiffer Craft Books on Related Subjects:**

*Tapestry with Pulled Warp: Inspiration, Technique, and the Creative Process,* Susan Iverson, ISBN 978-0-7643-6760-1

*Velvet on My Mind, Velvet on My Loom: Velvet Weaving Past & Present,* Wendy Landry, foreword by Louise Mackie, ISBN 978-0-7643-5934-7

*Weaving with Wire: Creating Woven Metal Fabric,* Christine K. Miller, ISBN 978-0-7643-6693-2



Library of Congress Control Number: 2026903899



Designed by Lori S. Malkin Ehrlich
Front cover design by Lindsay Hess
Type set in Adobe Caslon Pro / Proxima Nova
ISBN: 978-0-7643-7239-1
ePub: 978-1-5073-0758-8
Printed in India

10 9 8 7 6 5 4 3 2 1

MIX
Paper | Supporting responsible forestry
FSC™ C016779

Published by Schiffer Craft
An imprint of Schiffer Publishing, Ltd.
4880 Lower Valley Road
Atglen, PA 19310
Phone: (610) 593-1777; Fax: (610) 593-2002
Email: Info@schifferbooks.com
Web: www.schifferbooks.com

*To Barbara Elkins,*
*a fine weaver, and a person who*
*has been generous with time, ideas, and*
*support for more than thirty years.*

# CONTENTS

FOLLOWING SPREAD:

*The months ahead*, 48" × 79", linen, 2021, detail

the ... more ...

meant more anima

"They're good anima

r Lissy laughed at the sh

t seemed to find sweetness

hile Lissy saw only sillin

e worked among the sh "F

d behind the barn.

g

rd the house tha

id was not think

ep's abject
their odd yello
and he was ha
ep in the meado
a shepherd,"

# ACKNOWLEDGMENTS

I am indebted to the weavers who provided valuable comments on many aspects of the manuscript that has become this book. While any errors and inconsistencies are mine alone, each of these individuals has contributed enormously to the final result. My deepest thanks go to Kate Barber (www.katebarbertextiles.com), Eileen Crawford (former dean, Weavers' Guild of Boston), Chris Hammel (www.ekphrasisweaver.com), Lisa Hill (www.plainweave.net), Eric Frisino (www.comfortclothweaving.com), Tegan Frisino (www.comfortclothweaving.com), and Emily Gwynn (www.handstoworktextiles.com). As weavers they each continue to inspire me, and I encourage readers to seek out and explore their creativity in more detail.

Marthe Young, artist and sewist, provided the exquisite technical drawings for chapter 1, and equally fine sewing and assembly of the projects Bird Lover's Teatime, Neptune, and Mariner's Compass.

The photographer John Polak and the stylist Tracey Eller brought a high level of professionalism and dedication to the beautiful images that accompany the projects found in chapter 3. Unless noted, all additional photos are by John Polak.

Finally, most importantly, I want to express my love to Sonia Krotkov—for every reason, including her patience, kindness, and steadfast encouragement to spend my days doing what I care about the most.

# PROLOGUE

*It was the last hour of daylight, on the last day of the year.*

I was walking alone when those words suggested themselves to me, something I do regularly to gather myself and settle my brain. The words were musical, and their quiet rhythms sounded again and again in my mind as I walked.

*It was the last hour of daylight, on the last day of the year.*

The words were also evocative of ideas and feelings that are often with me: the beauty of winter, the turning of the seasons, things reaching their natural ends. Sometimes such words, coming at unsuspecting moments, tell us about who we are.

I wrote them down.

The next images came quickly: a young woman and her father caring for a newborn lamb, an aged ewe near death. The man was a weaver, himself recently widowed, his daughter grief-stricken at her mother's passing, acutely lonely despite her father's kindness. Their town was a rural place that was turning toward industrialization and modernity. The man worked at his loom ceaselessly.

The images added depth and texture to the rhythms of the first sentence. They spoke of beginnings as well as endings, and of the continuity to be found in compassion and enjoyable work, despite troubling and perhaps destructive changes on the horizon. The push and pull of the ideas was intriguing and hinted at an approaching crisis, but not something powerful and titanic, such as a clash between good and evil. Instead, the jostling of images carried a tension that was gentler—hope versus despair.

With those words and images my story had begun, although I didn't know how it would end. I still don't know. But it had given me something to weave.

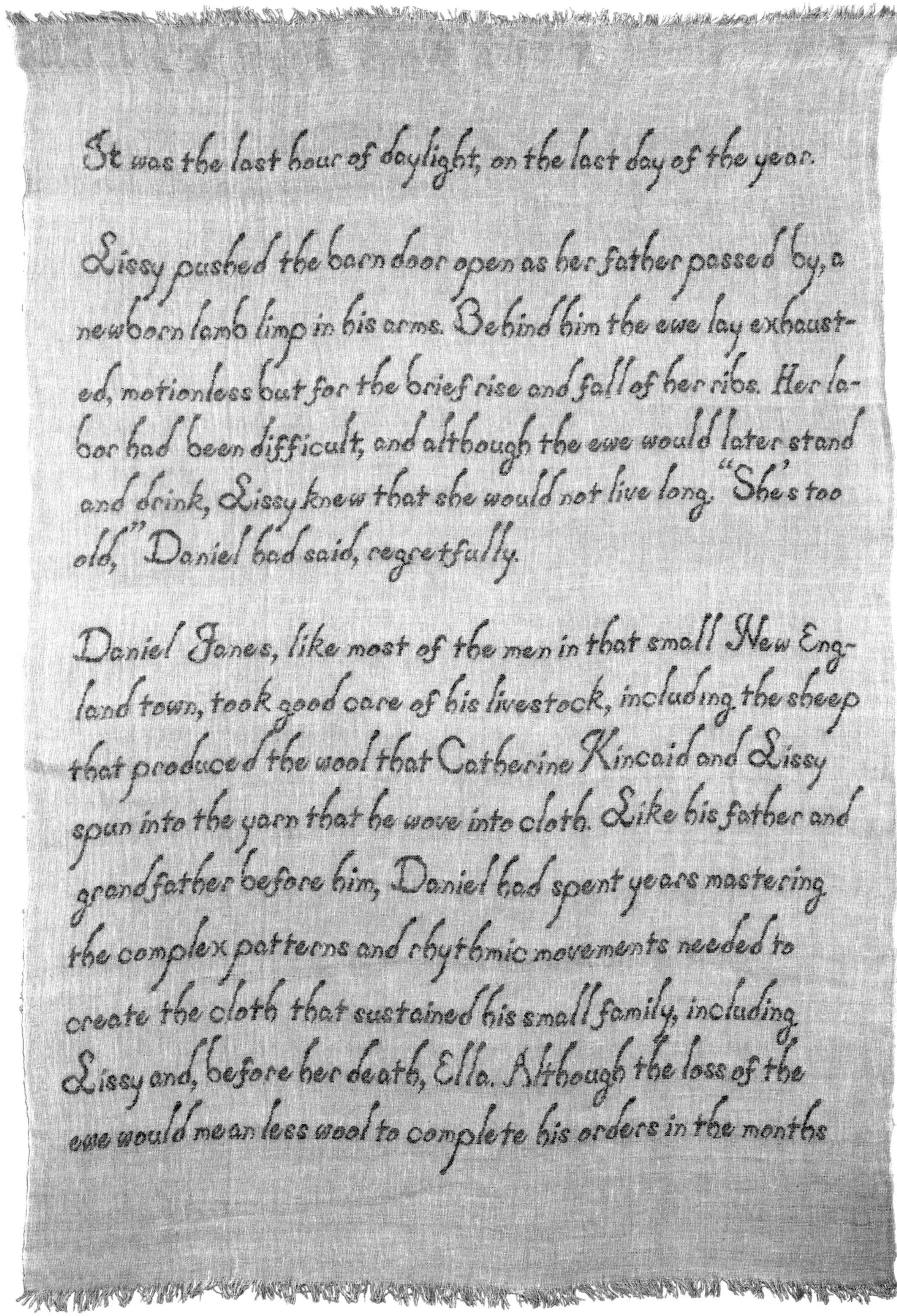

It was the last hour of daylight, on the last day of the year.

Lissy pushed the barn door open as her father passed by, a newborn lamb limp in his arms. Behind him the ewe lay exhausted, motionless but for the brief rise and fall of her ribs. Her labor had been difficult, and although the ewe would later stand and drink, Lissy knew that she would not live long. "She's too old," Daniel had said, regretfully.

Daniel Jones, like most of the men in that small New England town, took good care of his livestock, including the sheep that produced the wool that Catherine Kincaid and Lissy spun into the yarn that he wove into cloth. Like his father and grandfather before him, Daniel had spent years mastering the complex patterns and rhythmic movements needed to create the cloth that sustained his small family, including Lissy and, before her death, Ella. Although the loss of the ewe would mean less wool to complete his orders in the months

# INTRODUCTION

Woven inlay is a technique that allows a weaver to decorate cloth in ways that are free of the constraints inherent to the traditional four- and eight-harness looms that are commonly used by weavers today.

When weaving plain weave on such a loom, contrasting colors are typically found as stripes in the weft reaching from selvage to selvage, or extending the entire length of the warp. When the stripes intersect, they form plaids. That is the sum total of what a weaver can do with color when working on a four- or eight-harness loom, unless they find alternate ways to add color to the cloth. Woven inlay is one of those alternate ways. Other ways to add color freely to cloth include resist dyeing the warp or weft (or both), painting directly on the warp, and printing or embroidering finished cloth after it is woven. There are more techniques as well.

With woven inlay, the weaver inserts contrasting weft yarns anywhere in the cloth by hand, as freely and spontaneously as desired. Decorative patterns grow gradually from these inserted wefts as the weaving progresses. The weaver is not limited to stripes and plaids alone. The possibilities offered by numerous inlay techniques seem endless, even for weavers working with primitive looms. Of these techniques, brocade, dukagång, the Moorman technique, and a variety of "pick-up" weaves are among the most widely used.

At one end of the spectrum of inlay, the technique is a quick way to add color and pattern to items such as pillows, blankets, and scarves, often using relatively heavy yarns and uncomplicated designs. At the spectrum's other extreme, inlay furnishes a way to make cloth of extraordinary richness and complexity.

As a weaver of inlay, I fall to the simpler end of the spectrum. This might be the result of the limits of my imagination, or to the fact that, throughout my weaving life, I have found great satisfaction in commonplace types of cloth. Regardless of the reasons, nearly everything I make is plain weave, the most unassuming of fabrics. Weavers who share my straightforward approach will be happy to learn that the inlay I describe here is an easier version of the technique, no matter how intricate the final results may appear. At the same time, I hope that weavers who are drawn by complexity will find a foundation for their future experiments with inlay.

Over the years, there has been considerable interest in the role of mathematics in weaving, primarily the ways that weavers use mathematical equations to design patterns.* For me, math plays virtually no role in patternmaking or any other aspect of

**Accounts of the use of mathematics in weaving can be found in James Essinger,* Jacquard's Web: How a Hand Loom Led to the Birth of the Information Age *(Oxford: Oxford University Press, 2004); and Virginia Postrel,* The Fabric of Civilization: How Textiles Made the World *(New York: Basic Books, 2021).*

*It was the last hour of daylight*, 41" × 72", linen, 2020, collection of Anna Von Mertens and Chris Anderson

weaving. On the other hand, I have admired the shapes and sounds of letters and words seemingly forever, and the intrinsic power of words—their ability to express ideas, convey sentiment, and suggest meaning—has added immeasurably to their appeal in my mind. This book will explore a singular corner of the world of woven inlay: its use to add words to woven cloth.

Predictably perhaps, it was a book that spurred my transformation from a weaver of ordinary household linen to one who would become absorbed by inserting words into cloth. The book was *Johnny Tremain,* Esther Forbes's tale of an apprentice silversmith caught in the violence and danger of the American Revolution. I read it when I was very young, and I have read it again at other times in my life. Johnny himself is not a particularly likeable character, being surprisingly bitter for someone so young, and occasionally cruel. But as a young reader myself when I first encountered the book, I overlooked the dark side of his personality and focused instead on his courage, and his skill as a silversmith. The book's portrayal of Boston craftsmen in the 1770s caught my imagination, and the pages where Johnny sought advice from Paul Revere, a real-life silversmith as well as revolutionary hero, have remained vivid in my mind.

It was that vividness, as it lifted Johnny from the black-and-white page, showing him in his unpleasant yet honorable glory, that caused me to close the book one day and exclaim to Sonia, "It's good to read about a heroic silversmith, but why hasn't someone written a book about a heroic weaver?"*

Sonia had listened to similar complaints each time I read *Johnny Tremain*, and always responded with a smile or laugh. This time, she smiled again. Then she said, "You write it."

I was already an experienced weaver of inlay on the day when the words *It was the last hour of daylight* came to mind. For a year or two previously, a group of small inlay patterns—a circle that recalled a rising sun, a lantern beaming light while its handle rounded above, a fleur-de-lis, and a mysterious, rounded shape that sprouted hooks—had taken up most of my weaving hours. It was a time of uncertainty and exploration for me. I was transfixed by the forms as they emerged under my fingers, and I wove them continually as decorations for small towels and other items. On many levels, I was satisfied with my process and its results. But a quality was lacking in the cloth I made, and

* *Despite being a decent and caring man, Silas Marner does not meet my definition of heroic. I had not yet discovered Kester Woodseaves, the weaver in Mary Webb's novel* Precious Bane.

I couldn't find the words to describe what I missed. A restlessness stirred as I worked at my loom each day, and the feeling was exciting, but troubling as well. These uncertainties persisted alongside the pleasure that I felt when reading or listening to stories and poems aloud. I found myself thinking about words—how they're shaped, and how they sound when spoken—rather than patterns in cloth alone. My restlessness would fade somewhat as I thought about stories that I admired, and I began to muse about how those stories might affect the weaving I would do. One day I thought, "Maybe a story could be woven into cloth," and a sense of wholeness enveloped me.

I continued to walk alone, admiring the landscape and weather of our town, and continued to think about stories and weaving. I read *The Witch of Blackbird Pond*, Elizabeth George Speare's romantic novel about a headstrong girl in colonial Connecticut. I read *Calico Bush*, a story of an indentured servant in 18th-century Maine, written by Rachel Field. I waited, and a week passed, and another.

OPPOSITE: Roman letters, sample for *The months ahead*, 23" × 27", linen, 2021, detail

ABOVE: *Lamb*, 21" × 28", linen, 2024, detail

RIGHT: *Lissy Janes*, 18" × 28", linen, 2022, detail

the months ahead, the sheep and lambs meant more to Daniel than just wool.

"They're good animals," he would say, whenever Lissy laughed at the sheep's abject stupidity. Daniel seemed to find sweetness in their odd yellow eyes, while Lissy saw only silliness, and he was happiest when he worked among the sheep in the meadows that stretched behind the barn. "I'm a shepherd," he would say, smiling.

But as he walked toward the house that cold December day, Daniel was not thinking about the meadows, or the contentment he found when working among his flock. The lamb he carried had been born too early, to a ewe that soon would be dead, and with a long winter yet to come. Daniel was thinking about keeping the lamb warm through the night, and about helping her to survive until spring. Losing the ewe was bad enough. Daniel was determined not to lose her lamb as well.

Then I began to write:

*It was the last hour of daylight, on the last day of the year.*

*Lissy pushed the barn door open as her father passed by, a newborn lamb limp in his arms. Behind him the ewe lay exhausted, motionless but for the brief rise and fall of her ribs. Her labor had been difficult, and although the ewe would later stand and drink, Lissy knew that she would not live long. "She's too old," Daniel had said, regretfully.*

*Daniel Janes, like most of the men in their small New England town, took good care of his livestock, including the sheep that produced the wool that Catherine Kincaid and Lissy spun into the yarn that he wove into cloth. Like his father and grandfather before him, Daniel had spent years mastering the complex patterns and rhythmic movements needed to create the cloth that sustained his small family, including Lissy and, before her death, Ella. Although the loss of the ewe would mean less wool to complete his orders in the months ahead, the sheep and lambs meant more to Daniel than just wool. "They're good animals," he said, whenever Lissy laughed at the sheep's abject stupidity. Daniel seemed to find sweetness in their odd, yellow eyes, while Lissy saw only silliness, and he seemed happiest when he worked among the sheep in the meadows that stretched behind the barn. "I'm a shepherd," he would say, and he would smile.*

*But as he walked toward the house that cold December day, Daniel was not thinking about the meadows, or the happiness he found when working among his flock. The lamb he carried had been born too early, to a ewe that soon would be dead, and with a long winter yet to come. Daniel was thinking about keeping the lamb warm through the night, and about being certain that she survived until spring. Losing the ewe was bad enough. Daniel was determined not to lose her lamb as well.*

When I talk about inlay, I often say, "If you can design and weave a circle, you can design and weave anything." I knew I could lay in a circle, but could I lay in words and sentences, phrases and paragraphs? Could the words and phrases be shaped into a flowing, cursive script, like handwriting? Could they be made to resemble roughly formed roman letters, as if they were carved from wood? Would such words, woven into cloth, tell a story in a way that others would want to read? Did I have the ability and stamina to do this? Or would I appear foolish?

I found answers to some of those questions over the next weeks and months, yet I found more uncertainty as well. As the story came to life in my imagination, it began to introduce new narrative themes, new styles of lettering, and new illustrations to accompany the words I was writing. Each of these developments led to additional questions to be answered. Some of these new elements thrived, while others withered and died. I wasn't troubled by the loss of my less robust ideas, because I knew they would soon be replaced by others. I came to realize that to write a story and weave it into cloth was an entirely open-ended undertaking of endless possibilities, producing fresh ideas as readily as it produced anxiety and accidents. In that way at least, it resembled life.

The exhilaration of finding a story unfolding in my mind, the joy of seeing words and phrases appear in my cloth as I wove, the satisfaction of designing illustrations—a hen, a potbellied stove, a man holding a newborn lamb—has stayed with me in the ensuing years. While the story of a weaver and his daughter appears only briefly here, it is the basis of virtually everything I have woven since the day it presented itself. That story is also the foundation of everything written in the pages that follow.

*The months ahead*, 48" × 79", linen, 2021

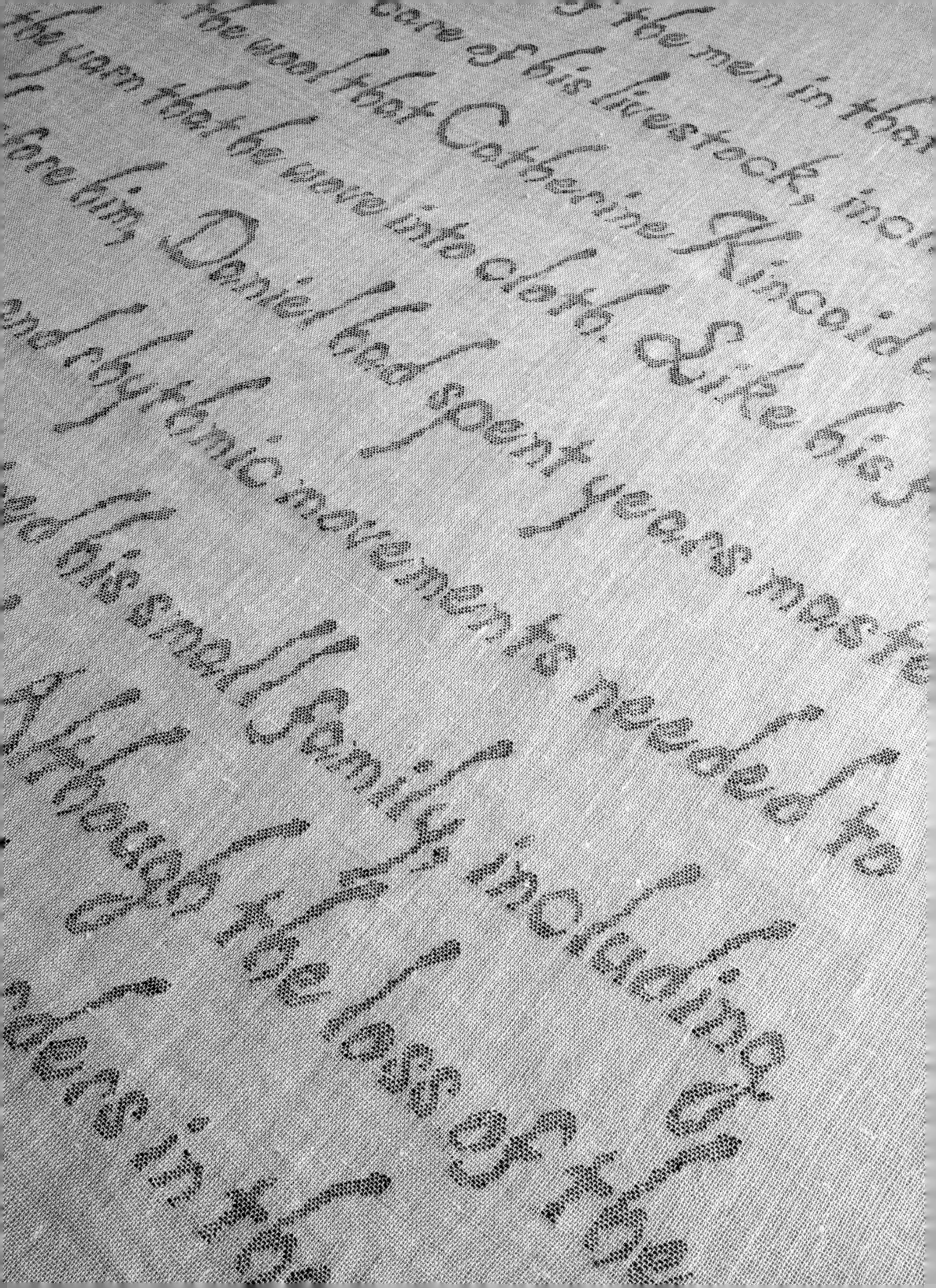

the men in that
care of his livestock, inc
the wool that Catherine Kincaid
yarn that he wove into cloth. Like his
fore him, Daniel had spent years maste
and rhythmic movements needed to
and his small family, including
Although the loss of
ders in the

— *Chapter 1* —

# WEAVING

## WOVEN INLAY'S BASIC FEATURES

1. When weaving inlay, one or more short lengths of additional weft are inserted by hand into an open *shed* (the opening in the warp that results when a harness is lifted). Among weavers, these inserted wefts are known as *supplemental wefts* and are described as having been *inlaid* or *laid in.* The process itself is called *laying in.* Depending on the context, a length of weft used to lay in a pattern will be called here a *pattern strand* or a *strand.* Collectively, those strands will be called the *pattern weft* or the *pattern.*

2. A background pick is thrown through the same shed as the pattern, spanning the entire width from selvage to selvage.

3. Laid-in patterns can be inserted anywhere in the cloth. In many cases a single pattern shape, such as a circle, a square, or a flower, placed directly in the center of the cloth, is satisfactory. In other cases, the freedom inherent to the technique encourages designs that grow and spread widely across the cloth, seemingly at will

4. Inlaid patterns can be developed spontaneously while weaving or can be guided by cartoons, marks painted or drawn on the warp, or written drafts prepared in advance. The technique shown here relies on written drafts, with every important design decision made prior to weaving.

5. The weaver is free to lay in the pattern on the front of the cloth or the back. (The front is the side that will be displayed to the viewer after it is removed from the loom. The front faces away from the weaver as they work at the loom, while the back faces toward the weaver.) Laying in on the back conceals the knots and other imperfections that are byproducts of the inlay process. Therefore, the method described here will be laying in on the back of the cloth.

6. Patterns laid in on the back will appear reversed when viewed on the front of the cloth. Simple shapes, such as circles or squares, or even more intricate shapes like a man holding a lamb are easily understood if reversed. However other patterns, such as words, are unintelligible when viewed backward. When laying in patterns of this kind, the weaver works from a draft showing the pattern in reverse, so that it is oriented correctly when seen from the front.

7. Patterns are laid in from bottom to top, regardless of whether they are worked on the front or the back of the cloth.

8. While laying in a pattern, the weaver counts raised *warp ends* (the individual threads making up the warp) of the open shed to guarantee that the pattern is being formed correctly.

9. A range of fibers and weights are suitable for woven inlay, depending on the final effect that is desired. Due to its strength, and the clarity of the laid-in patterns that can be achieved with finer weights of tightly spun yarns, 40/2 linen is the fiber used throughout this book.

## READING DRAFTS

1. Woven inlay is notated using a profile draft—that is, a draft that provides the details of the pattern to be laid in without showing the underlying structure of the cloth itself.

2. Profile drafts are typically graphed, with pencil on paper or digitally. Drafts graphed at 10 squares to the inch are easy to write and read, whether written on paper or a computer screen.

OPPOSITE:

*It was the last hour of daylight* detail

3. The plain-weave foundation is woven with a straight draw threading on four harnesses, using two sheds. For the first shed, the first (closest to the weaver) and third harnesses are lifted together; for the second shed, the second and fourth (farthest from the weaver) harnesses are lifted. Throughout this book, these two sheds will be called the 1–3 and 2–4 sheds. (A draft for plain weave with a straight draw threading can be found in the introduction to chapter 3.)

4. Every horizontal row of a draft represents a 1–3 shed.

5. The squares that make up the horizontal rows represent the raised warp ends of the 1–3 sheds. With plain weave as the foundation, this means that each horizontal row shows every second warp end only—that is, half of the warp.

6. Dots, squares, X's, or other symbols are inserted into squares in the draft to identify the raised warp ends under which the pattern weft is laid in.

7. The 2–4 sheds are not indicated in the drafts, and only the pattern strands being laid in within the 1–3 sheds are shown. This is because, to be "square," a draft must show the same number of *weft picks* (the individual threads inserted perpendicular to the warp ends) as warp ends. However, as noted in #5, the drafts presented here show only half of the warp ends. To remain square, the draft must show half of the weft picks as well.

   As it happens, the pattern in the 2–4 sheds serves only to connect one 1–3 shed to the next. Removing the 2–4 sheds in the drafts is an effective shorthand that reduces the number of weft picks by half, while shifting the responsibility for placing the pattern in those sheds to the weaver. To address that responsibility, the weaver will weigh a number of options to find the best linkage of the pattern from shed to shed. While that may sound stress-provoking, the choices for the 2–4 sheds are typically logical and straightforward. This process is explained fully in the next section.

## A GUIDE TO INLAY IN THE 2–4 SHEDS

Lines that angle to the right or left, vertical lines, horizontal lines, and lines that reverse direction to form curves are the basis for many designs, including the patterns in this book. These four types of lines will be used here as examples of how the pattern is usually laid in within the 1–3 sheds, followed by "next steps" demonstrating the likeliest ways to insert the pattern within the ensuing 2–4 sheds. Taken together, these examples and next steps offer a reliable method for placing the pattern in virtually every 2–4 shed.

Lines laid in to cloth are used in different ways. Most commonly, they are thin, linear marks that look as if they had been drawn with a pencil or pen. But a line can also be the edge of a shape that itself consists of laid-in color. For instance, in the project titled Bird Lover's Teatime (see page 79), thin, "drawn" lines outline the bird's breast, legs, and feet. Simultaneously, the rest of the shape, including the tail, back, and head, is defined by the edges of filled-in areas of color. The lines shown in the examples here can be understood to include both "drawn" lines, and lines as edges. The principles for laying in the pattern strands in the 2–4 sheds are the same, regardless of which type of line is being formed.

### Lines That Angle to the Right or Left

**Example 1.** In the first shed (a 1–3 shed), a pattern strand is passed under a single raised warp end (fig. 1, shed 1). In the third shed (also a 1–3 shed), the strand will pass under the raised warp end offset to the left by one from the warp end used in the first shed (fig. 1, shed 3). Repeating this motion will make a line that angles to the left.

**Next step:** Continue the angled line to the left by passing the strand in the second shed (a 2–4 shed) under the raised warp end immediately to the left of the warp end used for the pattern in the first shed (fig. 1, shed 2).

**Example 2.** The steps are reversed when the movement of the line is to the right. In the first shed, a pattern strand is passed under a single raised warp end (fig. 2, shed 1). In the third shed, the

Fig. 1.

strand will pass under the raised warp end offset to the right by one from the warp end used in the first shed (fig. 2, shed 3). Repeating this motion will make a line that angles to the right.

**Next step:** Continue the angled line to the right by passing the strand in the second shed under the raised warp end immediately to the right of the warp end used for the pattern in the first shed (fig. 2, shed 2).

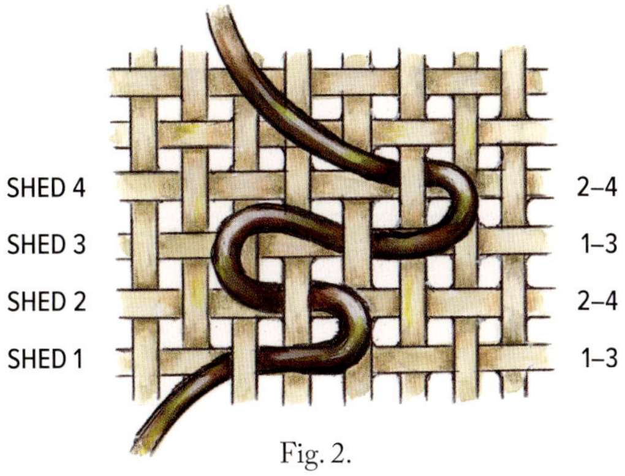


Fig. 2.

**Example 3.** The steps remain the same when the pattern strand is passed under two or more raised warp ends in the 1–3 sheds. For example:

In the first shed, a pattern strand is passed under two raised warp ends side by side (fig. 3a, shed 1). In the third shed, the strand will pass under two raised warp ends offset to the left by one (fig. 3a, shed 3).

**Next step:** Continue the angled line to the left by passing the strand in the second shed under the raised warp end immediately to the left of the right-hand warp end used for the pattern in the first shed, then under the next warp end to the left (two warp ends total; fig. 3a, shed 2).

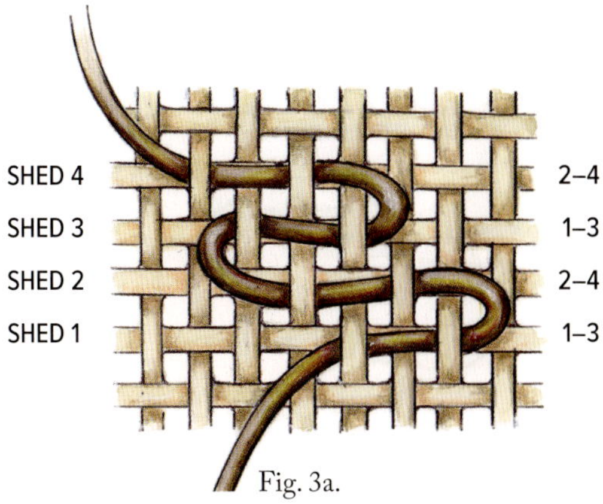


Fig. 3a.

The procedure is reversed when the movement is to the right (fig. 3b).

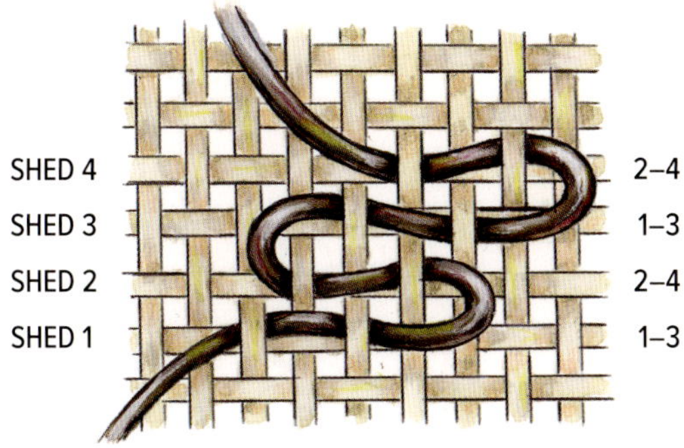


Fig. 3b.

The same steps are followed regardless of the number of warp ends under which the pattern is inserted. For example:

In the first shed, the pattern strand is passed under six raised warp ends side by side (fig. 3c, shed 1). In the third shed, the strand will pass under six raised warp ends offset to the right by one (fig. 3c, shed 3).

**Next step:** Continue the angled line to the right by passing the strand in the second shed under the raised warp end immediately to the right of the right-hand warp end used for the pattern in the first shed, then under the next five warp ends to the left (six warp ends total; fig. 3c, shed 2).

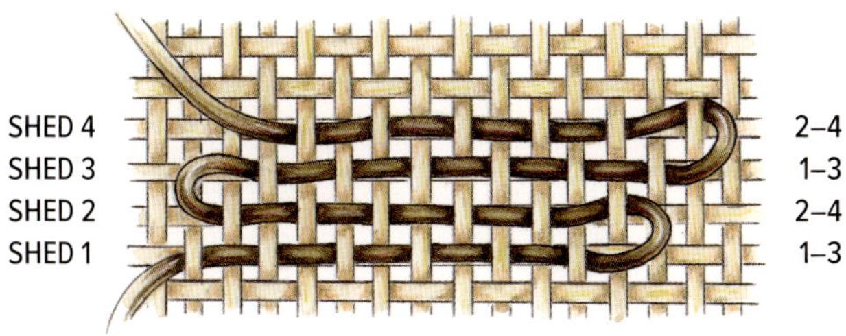


Fig. 3c.

**Example 4.** Unlike the lines seen in the previous examples, other lines move irregularly. For example:

In the first shed, a pattern strand is passed under two raised warp ends side by side (fig. 4, shed 1).

In the third shed, the strand will pass under eight raised warp ends offset to the left by one (fig. 4, shed 3).

In the fifth shed, the strand will pass under a single raised warp end offset to the left by one (fig. 4, shed 5).

**Next step:** Link the first and third sheds by passing the strand in the second shed under the raised warp end immediately to the left of the right-hand warp end used for the pattern in the first shed, then under the next warp end to the left (two warp ends total; fig. 4, shed 2). Note that a long pattern float will occur between the second and third sheds. To address this problem, see "Preventing Floats in the Pattern Weft" (page 40) and "Carrying Over" (page 41).

Link the third and fifth sheds by passing the strand in the fourth shed under the raised warp end immediately to the left of the right-hand warp end used for the pattern in the third shed, then under the next seven warp ends to the left (eight warp ends total; fig. 4, shed 4).

In the sixth shed, pass the strand under the single raised warp end immediately to the left of the warp end used for the pattern in the fifth shed (fig. 4, shed 6).

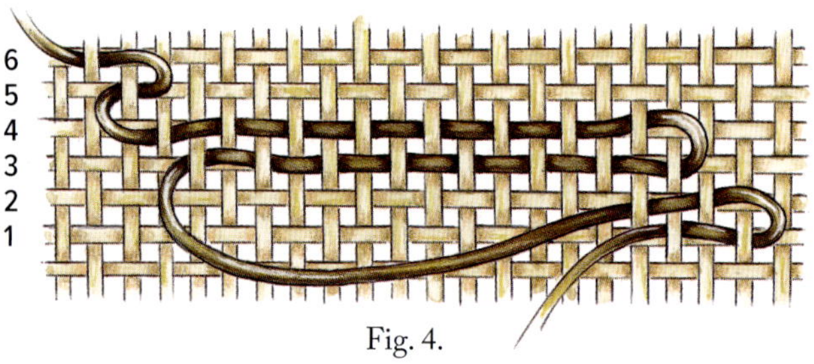


Fig. 4.

**Example 5.** Wedge-like pattern shapes expand outward to the right and left. For example:

In the first shed, the pattern strand is passed under a single raised warp end (fig. 5, shed 1). In the third shed, the strand will pass under three raised warp ends side by side, including the warp ends offset to the left and right by one from the warp end used for the pattern in the first shed (fig. 5, shed 3).

**Next step:** Begin the outward movement of the shape in the second shed by passing the strand under the raised warp end immediately to the right of the warp end used for pattern in the first shed, then under the next warp end to the left (two warp ends in total; fig. 5, shed 2).

Fig. 5.

This will be the same regardless of the number of raised warp ends used for the pattern in each 1–3 shed—such as when two raised warp ends are used for the pattern in the first 1–3 shed, followed by four in the second 1–3 shed, or when three raised warp ends are used for the pattern in the first 1–3 shed, followed by five in the second 1–3 shed, etc.

**Example 6.** Other wedge-like pattern shapes taper inward. For example:

In the first shed, a pattern strand is passed under three raised warp ends side by side (fig. 6, shed 1). In the third shed, the strand will pass under a single raised warp, which is the middle of the three warp ends used for the pattern in the first shed (fig. 6, shed 3).

**Next step:** Begin the inward movement of the shape in the second shed by passing the strand under the raised warp end immediately to the left of the right-hand warp end used for the pattern in the first shed, then under the next warp end to the left (two warp ends in total; fig. 6, shed 2).

Fig. 6.

**Example 7.** A tapering movement can occur when a vertical line shifts to the right or left. For example:

In the first shed, a pattern strand is passed under two raised warp ends side by side (fig. 7a, shed 1). In the third shed, the strand will pass under the raised warp end that was the left-hand warp end used for the pattern in the first shed (fig. 7a, shed 3).

**Next step:** Begin the tapering motion in the second shed by passing the strand under the raised warp end immediately to the left of the right-hand warp end used for the pattern in the first shed (fig. 7a, shed 2).

Fig. 7a.

The steps are reversed when the movement is to the right (fig. 7b).

Fig. 7b.

## Vertical Lines

**Example 8.** In the first shed, a pattern strand is passed under a single raised warp end (figs. 8a, b, c; shed 1). In the third shed, the strand will pass under the same raised warp end as that of the pattern in the first shed (figs. 8a, b, c; shed 3). Repeating this motion will make a vertical line.

**Next step:** There are three options in the second shed.

First option: Link the first and third sheds by passing the strand in the second shed under the raised warp end immediately to the left of the warp end used for the pattern in the first shed. Repeating this motion will make a vertical line that "zigs" left (fig. 8a, shed 2).

Second option: Link the first and third sheds by passing the strand in the second shed under the raised warp end immediately to the right of the warp end used for the pattern in the first shed, making a line that "zigs" right (fig. 8b, shed 2).

Third option: Link the first and third sheds by passing the strand in the second shed under the raised warp end immediately to the right of the warp end used for the pattern in the first shed, then under the next warp end to the left (two warp ends in total; fig. 8c, shed 2). Repeating this motion will make a stable line that is broader in profile than the lines in figs. 8a and 8b.

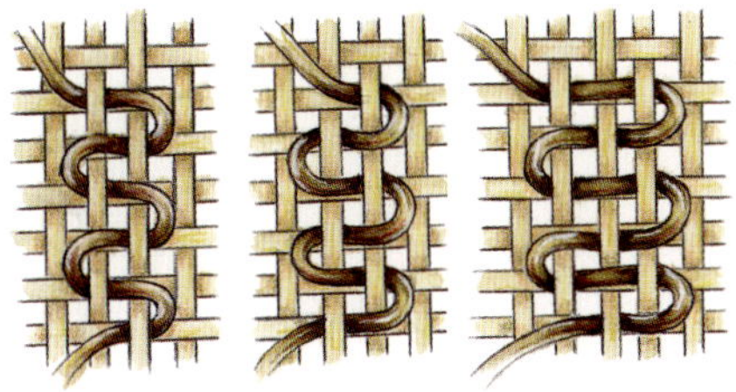


Fig. 8a-b-c.

**Example 9.** The same procedure is followed when a pattern strand is passed under two or more raised warp ends in the 1–3 sheds. For example:

In the first shed, a pattern strand is passed under five raised warp ends side by side (figs. 9a, b, c, d; shed 1). In the third shed, the strand will pass under the same five raised warp ends as those used for the pattern in the first shed (figs. 9a, b, c, d; shed 3).

**Next step:** Again, there are multiple options in the second shed.

First option: Link the first and third sheds by passing the strand in the second shed under the raised warp end immediately to the left of the right-hand warp end used for the pattern in the first shed, then under the next four warp ends to the left (five warp ends total; fig. 9a, shed 2). Repeating this motion will make a vertical line that "zigs" left.

Fig. 9a.

Second option: Link the first and third sheds by passing the strand in the second shed under the raised warp end immediately to the right of the right-hand warp end used for the pattern in the first shed, then under the next four warp ends to the left (five warp ends total; fig. 9b, shed 2). Repeating this motion will make a vertical line that "zigs" right.

Fig. 9b.

Third option: Link the first and third sheds by passing the strand in the second shed under the raised warp end immediately to the right of the right-hand warp end used for the pattern in the first shed, then under the next five warp ends to the left (six warp ends total; fig. 9c, shed 2). Repeating this motion will make a stable line that expands outward slightly with each 2–4 shed.

Fig. 9c.

Fourth option: Link the first and third sheds by passing the strand in the second shed under the raised warp end immediately to the left of the right-hand warp end used for the pattern in the first shed, then under the next three warp ends to the left (four warp ends total; fig. 9d, shed 2). Repeating this motion will make a stable line that draws inward slightly with each 2–4 shed.

Fig. 9d.

### Horizontal Lines

Horizontal lines are typically slender in shape and encompass two or four sheds only. Such lines are frequently followed by lines that extend upward from one or both ends, to form squares, rectangles, or other shapes.

**Example 10.** In the first shed, a pattern strand is passed under seven raised warp ends (fig. 10, shed 1). In the third shed, the existing strand will pass under a single raised warp end offset to the left by one from the left-hand warp end used for the pattern in the first shed (fig. 10, shed 3, left). At the right of the shape, a new strand is introduced in the third shed that passes under a single raised warp end offset to the right by one from the right-hand warp end used for the pattern in the first shed (fig. 10, shed 3, right).

**Next step:** Begin the outward movement of the shape by passing the strand in the second shed under the raised warp end immediately to the right of the right-hand warp end used for the pattern in the first shed, then under the next seven warp ends to the left (eight warp ends total;

Fig. 10.

fig. 10, shed 2). [To address the long pattern floats that may occur when laying in horizontal lines, see "Preventing Floats in the Pattern Weft" (page 40) and "Carrying Over" (page 41).]

### Lines That Curve

Curving lines typically combine angled lines with horizontal or vertical lines (fig. 11). Therefore, the steps for laying in the pattern in every 2–4 shed of a curving line can be found in the descriptions of "Lines That Angle to the Right or Left," "Vertical Lines," and "Horizontal Lines," *above*. The steps for drafting curving lines are described in chapter 2.

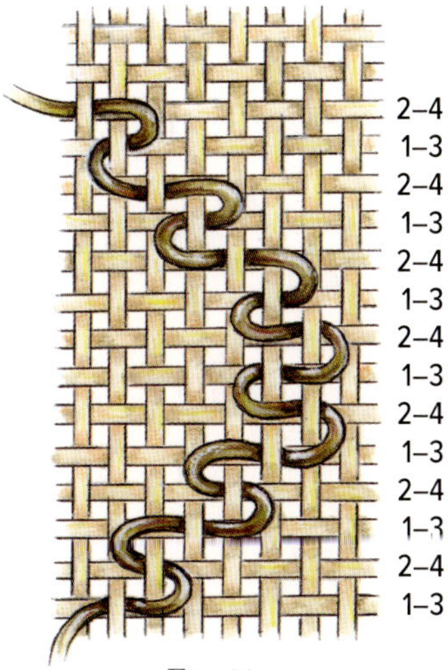


Fig. 11.

## LAYING IN: CHOOSING THE TEXT STYLE

To weave words into cloth, you start with the letters. The English alphabet includes twenty-six letters, with each letter found in in both upper and lower cases. This means that a total of fifty-two characters are needed.

That was my challenge when I started work on a laid-in version of the text that began with the words *It was the last hour of daylight*. Each letter had to be designed on paper, translated into a draft, and woven as a sample, with some of the letters likely to be sampled several times before being finished. The letters needed to be reasonably consistent in size and shape, so that they would fit together easily. They needed to be challenging to weave, so that they would hold my interest, but not so difficult that I would become frustrated. And they needed to be beautiful, because no one wants to weave something that is unattractive.

The style of the lettering had to be identified before I could begin. Ordinary, everyday lettering would be best for the plainspoken story I was telling, so I ruled out elaborate or ornamental styles. Given that my story takes place in the early 19th century, I disregarded styles such as gothic blackletter or the various Bauhaus letters that evoke other time periods. I also ruled out styles that are demanding to read—again, blackletter—or too highly detailed for my method of inlay. I was in search of a "face," as called by typographers, that was simple, evocative of early America, and interesting.

When those criteria became clear, the question of style was easily answered. Of the various letterings that I imagined, none met the requirements of simplicity, historicism, and beauty as readily as handwriting, particularly the flowing, graceful style known as "cursive." For years, I had admired examples of cursive writing that I saw in reproductions of 18th-century manuscripts and ledgers, but I knew little about its formal structure beyond its most obvious characteristics—it sloped to the right, the letters joined (or nearly joined) together, and the individual lines were of varying thicknesses, which I assumed to be the result of the natural rotation of an old-fashioned, square-edged quill or reed pen as the writer's hand moved over the page.

While there are difficulties to be addressed when designing and weaving letters and words into cloth, we're in luck here—because woven inlay has characteristics that lend themselves well to such matters. For example, cursive writing consists entirely of vertical lines, horizontal lines, and lines that angle or curve—lines that are identical to the lines described in the previous section. When laying in such lines, any degree of angle is possible, and the thickness or thinness of a line can be changed at any time—again, like handwriting. Furthermore, with inlay, two or more lines can be arranged to mirror each other, forming circles, squares, triangles, and diamonds, shapes that are the origins of many written letters. To look beyond the shapes of letters and words is to find that virtually any inlaid pattern can be made from these few design elements, including human figures, animals, trees, and flowers, as well as abstract patterns and other shapes not drawn from the world around us.

Inspired by the prospect of designing my own alphabet, I examined collections of 18th- and 19th-century handwriting, including the extraordinary penmanship displayed in Alfred Fairbank's *A Book of Scripts*. I came to appreciate the uniqueness of the English alphabet, with some of the letters appearing modest and inconsequential—the letter *o* comes to mind—while others looked dauntingly complicated. One of the alphabet's most commonly used letters is the first: *A*. And so, as I began to draw the alphabet that I would use to create a flowing inlaid script (which evolved over time as an italic rather than cursive style), I started at the alphabet's beginning—the lowercase *a* (fig. 12).

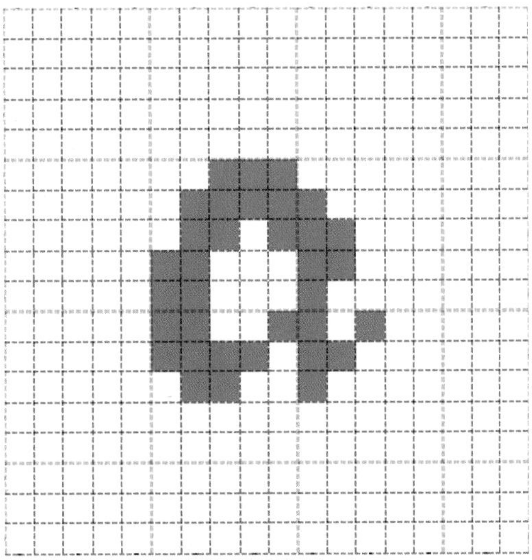

Fig. 12.

## LAYING IN THE LOWERCASE *a*

A step-by-step description of the process to lay in the lowercase italic *a* from beginning to end provides a good way to show the many decisions to be made during the laying-in process. While our focus here is on a single letter, this method can be applied to any letter of the alphabet—or, indeed, to any laid-in shape of any kind.

Note that only the 1–3 sheds are indicated in figs. 13, 16, 19, 23, 25, 28, 32, and 34. (For an explanation, see "Reading Drafts," #7, above.) This is reflected in the numbering of the sheds at the left of each of these figures.

The convention here is that the pattern strands will be passed from left to right in the 1–3 sheds, and right to left in the 2–4 sheds.

### The First 1–3 Shed (Shed 1, Fig. 13)

Open the first 1–3 shed. Mark the center of the warp. Then mark the design's center in the draft, shown as a vertical red line in fig. 13. (As with all letters and words here, the lowercase *a* in fig. 13 is reversed.)

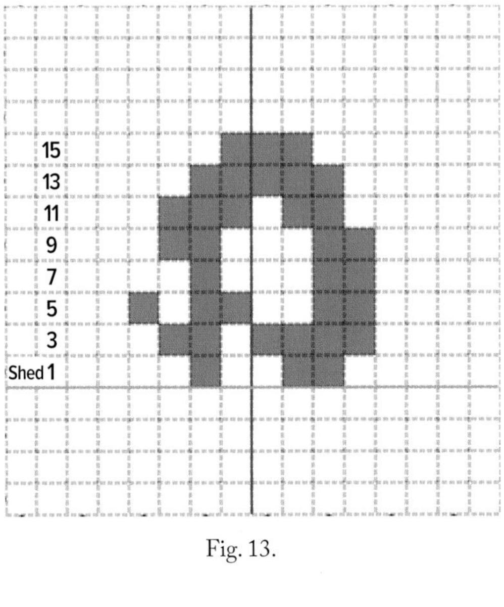


Fig. 13.

As indicated in the draft, begin by passing a pattern strand under the second raised warp end to the left of center. Leave a short, 1-inch "tail" at the left and bring the remainder of the strand upward to the right to be carried over to the next shed (see "Carrying Over," page 41).

Pass a second pattern strand under the second and third raised warp ends to the right of center. Leave a tail and bring the remainder of the strand upward to be carried over.

Double-check for accuracy, then secure each tail with a knot or loop. (For a description of knotting and looping, see "Durability," page 40.)

Throw a pick of background yarn in the same shed, beat the pattern strands and the background pick together, close the shed, and open the 2–4 shed.

### Laying In the 2–4 Shed (Shed 2)

On the right, note the wedge-like pattern shape that forms between sheds 1 and 3. Refer to example 5 of "A Guide to Inlay in the 2–4 Sheds." Pass the pattern strand into shed 2, under the raised warp end immediately to the right of the right-hand warp end used for the pattern in shed 1, then under the next two warp ends to the left (three warp ends in total; fig. 14).

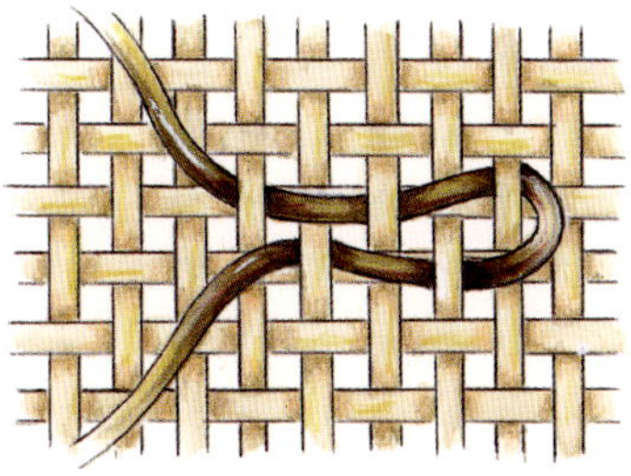


Fig. 14.

On the left, note the angled line that forms between sheds 1 and 3. Refer to example 1 of "A Guide to Inlay . . . ," then pass the pattern strand into shed 2, under the raised warp end immediately to the left of the warp end used for the pattern in shed 1 (fig. 15).

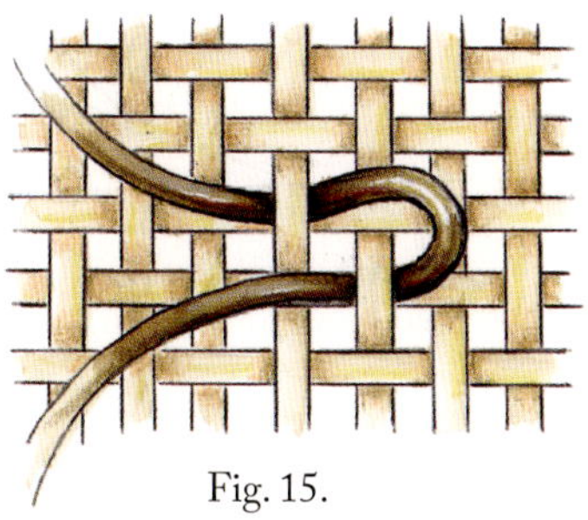


Fig. 15.

Bring both pattern strands upward to be carried over, then throw a pick of background yarn, beat, close the shed, and open the second 1–3 shed.

### The Second 1–3 Shed (Shed 3, Fig. 16)

On the left, pass the pattern strand under the second and third raised warp ends to the left of the center.

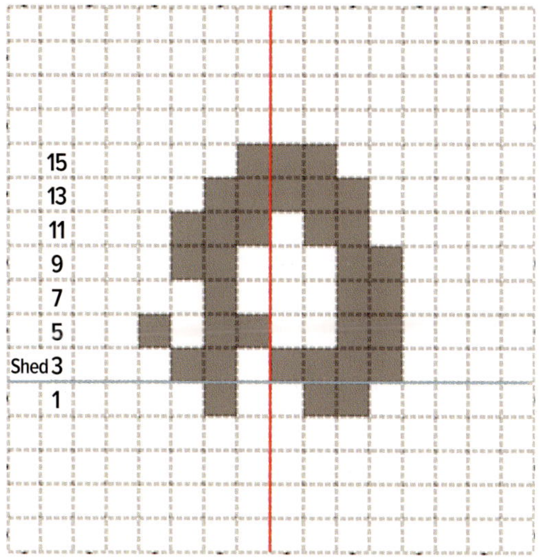


Fig. 16.

On the right, pass the pattern strand under the four raised warp ends to the right of center.

Bring both pattern strands upward, throw a pick of background yarn, beat, close the shed, and open the 2–4 shed.

### Laying In the 2–4 Shed (Shed 4)

On the right, note the vertical line that forms at the edge of the pattern in sheds 3, 5, 7, and 9. A line that "zigs" right would expand the rounded shape of the lowercase *a* in a way that seems appropriate to this letter. Refer to example 9 of "A Guide to Inlay . . ." In shed 4, pass the strand under the raised warp end immediately to the right of the right-hand warp end used for the pattern in shed 3, then under the next three warp ends to the left (four warp ends in total; fig. 17).

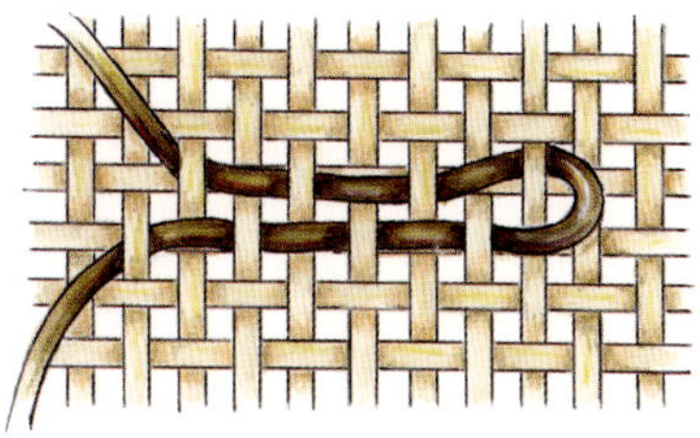


Fig. 17.

Continuing with shed 4, note the wedge-like pattern shape that forms on the left between sheds 3 and 5. Refer to example 5 of "A Guide to Inlay . . ." (page 20). Pass the strand under the raised warp end immediately to the right of the right-hand warp end used for the pattern in shed 3, then under the next two warp ends to the left (three warp ends in total; fig. 18).

Fig. 18.

Bring both pattern strands upward, throw a pick of the background yarn, beat, close the shed, and open the third 1–3 shed.

### The Third 1–3 Shed (Shed 5, Fig. 19)

Three pattern strands are needed for shed 5, located at the left, center, and right respectively, as follows:

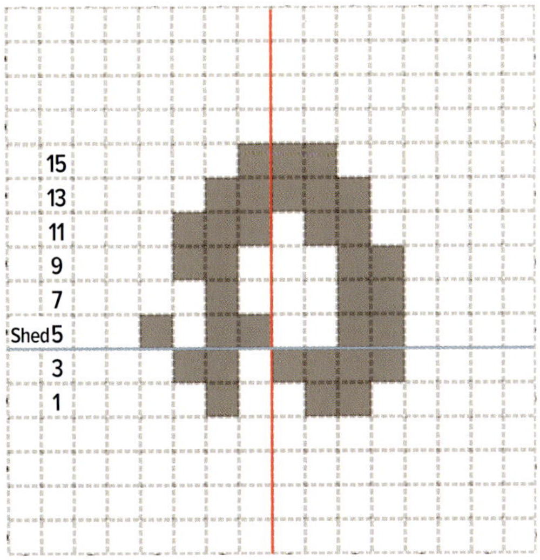


Fig. 19.

On the left, pass the existing strand under the single raised warp end immediately to the left of the warp end used for the pattern in the 2–4 shed just completed.

At the center, insert a new pattern strand under the two raised warp ends immediately to the left of the center and secure it with a knot or loop.

On the right, pass the existing strand under the third and fourth raised warp ends to the right of center. Note that the strand spans two raised warp ends before entering the open shed, leaving a short, acceptable float.

Bring the three pattern strands upward, throw a pick of the background yarn, beat, close the shed, and open the 2–4 shed.

### Laying In the 2–4 Shed (Shed 6)

On the right, refer to example 9 of "A Guide to Inlay . . ." Continue the vertical line that began in shed 3 by passing the strand into Shed 6, under the raised warp end immediately to the right of the right-hand warp end used for pattern in shed 5, then under the next warp end to the left (two warp ends total; fig. 20, shed 6).

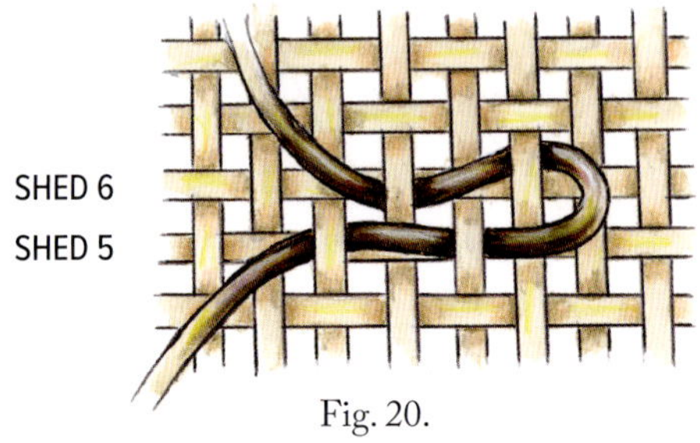


Fig. 20.

At the center, note the tapering motion that occurs between sheds 5 and 7. Refer to example 7 of "A Guide to Inlay . . . ," then pass the strand into shed 6, under the single raised warp end immediately to the left of the right-hand warp end used for the pattern in shed 5 (fig. 21).

Fig. 21.

On the left, refer to example 1 of "A Guide to Inlay . . ." Continue the angled line by passing the strand into shed 6, under the raised warp end immediately to the left of the warp end used for the pattern in shed 5. Because this action completes this part of the letter, the strand can be secured and trimmed (fig. 22). Then prepare for the fourth 1–3 shed as before.

Fig. 22.

### The Fourth 1–3 Shed (Shed 7, Fig. 23)

On the left, pass the pattern strand under the raised warp end immediately to the left of the warp end used for the pattern in the 2–4 shed just completed. (This strand was previously the center strand of shed 5.)

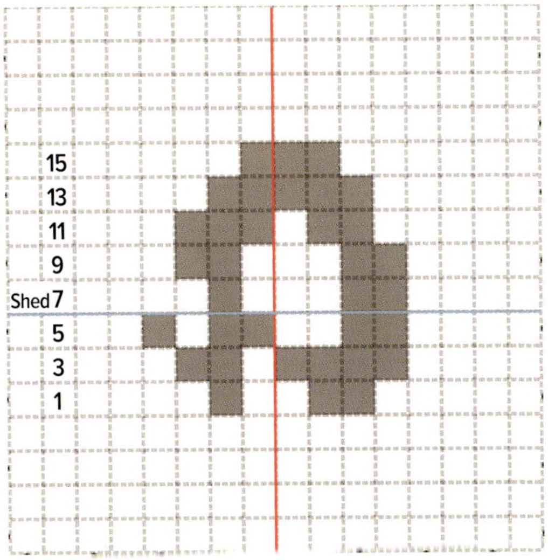


Fig. 23.

On the right, pass the strand under the same two raised warp ends that were used for the pattern in the previous 1–3 shed. Then prepare for the 2–4 shed as before.

### Laying In the 2–4 Shed (Shed 8)

On the right, refer to example 9 of "A Guide to Inlay . . ." Continue the vertical line that began in shed 3 by passing the strand under the raised warp end immediately to the right of the right-hand warp end used for pattern in shed 7, then under the next warp end to the left (two warp ends total; this movement is identical to the movement shown in fig. 20).

(b) On the left, note the angled line that forms between sheds 7 and 9. Refer to example 1 of "A Guide to Inlay . . . ," then pass the strand into shed 8, under the single raised warp end immediately to the left of the warp end used for the pattern in shed 7 (fig. 24). Then prepare for the fifth 1–3 shed as before.

Fig. 24.

### The Fifth 1–3 Shed (Shed 9, Fig. 25)

On the left, pass the pattern strand under the raised warp end immediately to the left of the warp end used for the pattern in the 2–4 shed just completed, then under the next warp end to the right (two warp ends in total).

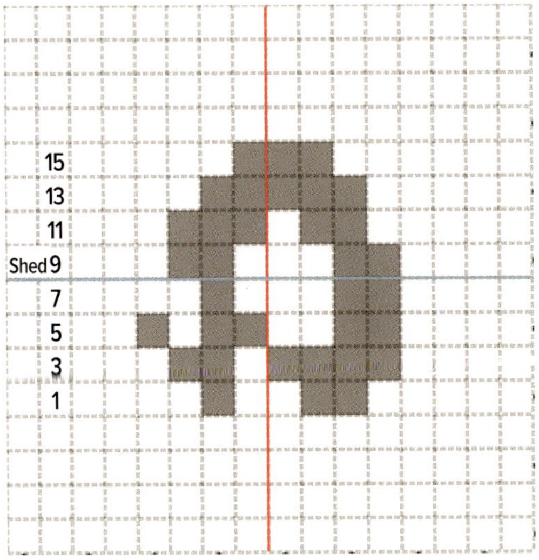


Fig. 25.

On the right, pass the strand under the same two raised warp ends that were used for the pattern in the previous 1–3 sheds. Then prepare for the 2–4 shed as before.

### Laying In the 2–4 Shed (Shed 10)

On the right, refer to example 3 of "A Guide to Inlay . . ." As the letter begins to narrow toward its apex, pass the pattern strand into shed 10, under the raised warp end immediately to the left of the right-hand warp end used for the pattern in shed 9, then under the next warp end to the left (two warp ends total; fig. 26).

Fig. 26.

On the left, refer to example 3 of "A Guide to Inlay . . ." Pass the strand into shed 10, under the raised warp end immediately to the right of the right-hand warp end used for the pattern in shed 9, then under the next warp end to the left (two warp ends total; fig. 27). Then prepare for the sixth 1–3 shed.

Fig. 27.

### The Sixth 1–3 Shed (Shed 11, Fig. 28)

On the left, pass the pattern strand under the same raised warp ends that were used for the pattern in the 1–3 shed of shed 9, then under the next warp end to the right (three warp ends in total).

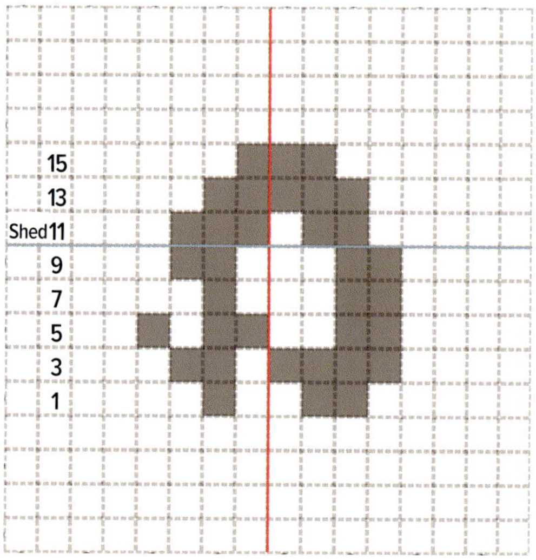


Fig. 28.

On the right, pass the pattern strand under the raised warp end immediately to the left of the left-hand warp end used for the pattern in the 2–4 shed just completed, then under the next warp end to the right (two warp ends in total). Then prepare for the 2–4 shed.

### Laying In the 2–4 Shed (Shed 12)

On the right, refer to example 3 of "A Guide to Inlay . . ." As the letter continues to narrow, pass the pattern strand into shed 12, under the raised warp end immediately to the left of the right-hand warp end used for the pattern in shed 11, then under the next warp end to the left (two warp ends total; fig. 29). Because this action completes this part of the letter, the strand can be secured and trimmed.

Fig. 29.

On the left, refer to example 6 of "A Guide to Inlay . . ." Create a wedge-like shape that tapers inward by passing the strand into shed 12, under the raised warp end immediately to the left of the right-hand warp end used for the pattern in shed 11, then under the next warp end to the left (two warp ends total; fig. 30). Then prepare for the seventh 1–3 shed.

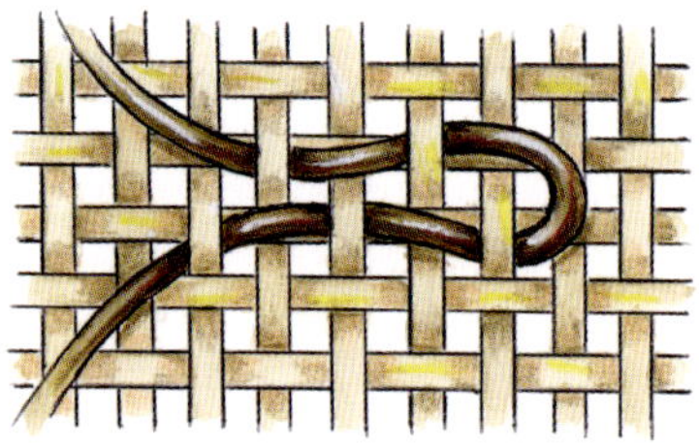


Fig. 30.

Alternately, as the letter continued to narrow, you might have carried the strand into shed 12, under the raised warp end immediately to the right of the right-hand warp end used for the pattern in shed 11, then under the next two warp ends to

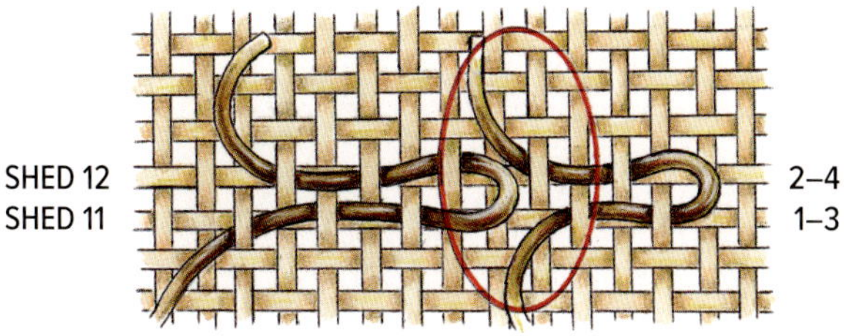


Fig. 31.

the left (three warp ends total; fig. 31). However, that would leave no raised warp ends without pattern to separate the left and right strands in shed 12, reducing the clarity of the shape when seen from the front, as highlighted in red in fig. 31. For more on this topic, see "Letters with Tight Spaces," page 34).

## The Seventh 1–3 Shed (Shed 13, Fig. 32)

Pass the single remaining pattern strand under five raised warp ends in total, including the two raised warp ends immediately to the right of the warp ends used for the pattern in the 2–4 shed just completed, as well as the next three raised warp ends to the right.

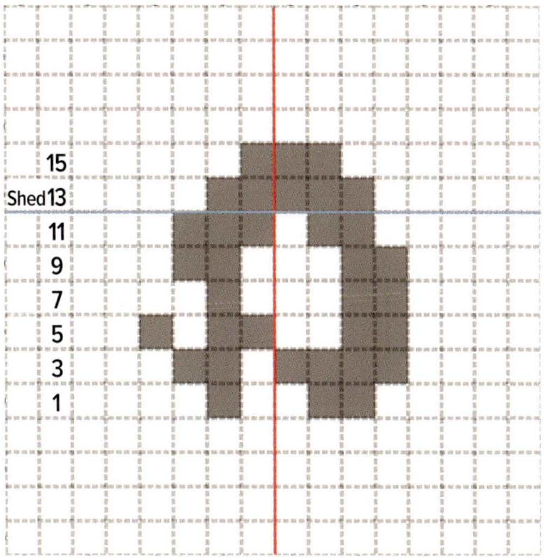


Fig. 32.

## Laying In the 2–4 Shed (Shed 14)

Refer to example 6 of "A Guide to Inlay . . ." Create a wedge-like shape that tapers inward by passing the strand into shed 14, under the raised warp end immediately to the left of the right-hand warp end used for the pattern in shed 13, then under the

Fig. 33.

next three warp ends to the left (four warp ends total; fig. 33).

## The Eighth 1–3 Shed (Shed 15, Fig. 34)

Pass the pattern strand under the three raised warp ends lifted directly between the four warp ends used for the pattern in the 2–4 shed just completed.

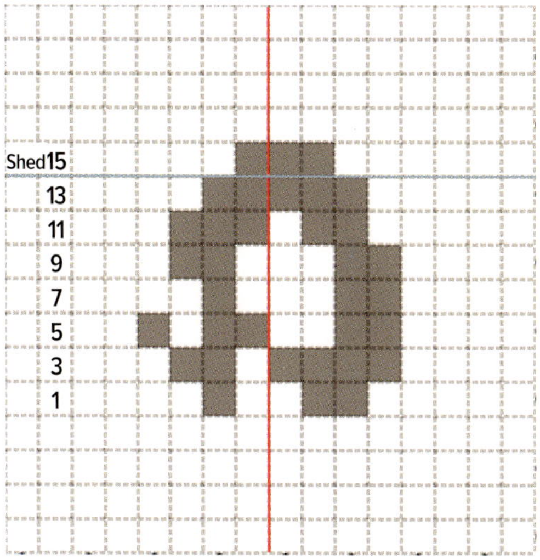


Fig. 34.

## Laying In the 2–4 Shed (Shed 16)

As before, refer to example 6 of "A Guide to Inlay . . ." Complete the letter by passing the pattern strand into shed 16, under the raised warp end immediately to the left of the right-hand warp end used for the pattern in shed 15, then under the next warp end to the left (two warp ends total; fig. 35). Then secure and trim the strand.

Fig. 35.

## WHAT'S AFTER *a*: LAYING IN OTHER LETTERS

While the process for laying in the letters of the alphabet is identical from one letter to the next, the letters themselves are highly varied, and some require more concentration and persistence than others. Although such letters may try our patience, they are also among the most interesting letters we have, and the English alphabet would be poorer without them. Here are some of the most common of these attention-seeking yet often charming letters.

### Letters with Descenders

Most letters in the English alphabet are positioned on the same horizontal plane (fig. 36).

But other letters do not fit this mold. The best known of these letters are those with descenders that fall below the horizontal plane, including *g*, *j*, *p*, *q*, and *y* (fig. 37).

There are additional letters that are usually found on the same plane as the others, but that stray occasionally below the line. Such letters include the lowercase *f* and the uppercase *J* and *Q* (fig. 38).

You will decide on the appropriate alignment for letters that fall below the horizontal plane as you prepare your draft. While weaving, however, the laying in of a descender can be a problem, because the descenders often begin early in the process,

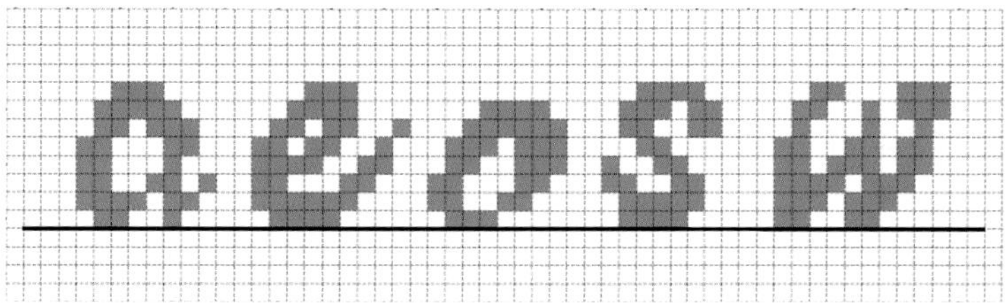

Fig. 36.

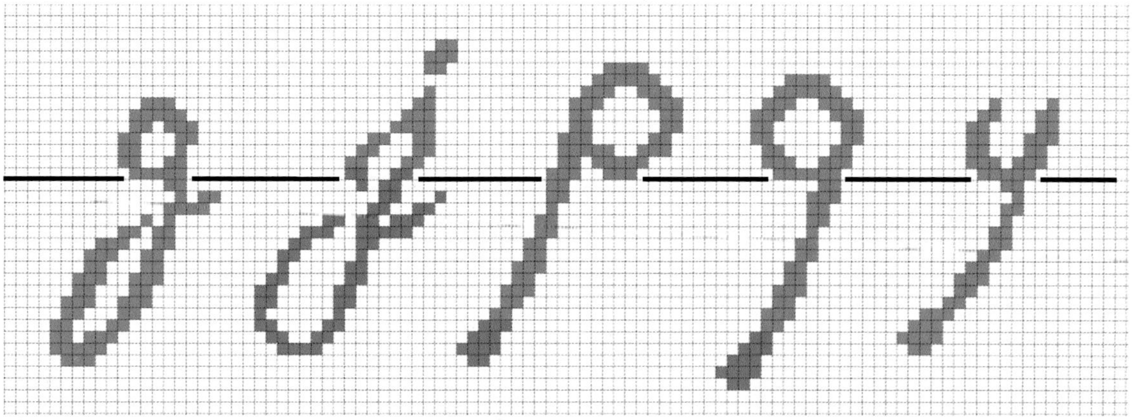

Fig. 37.

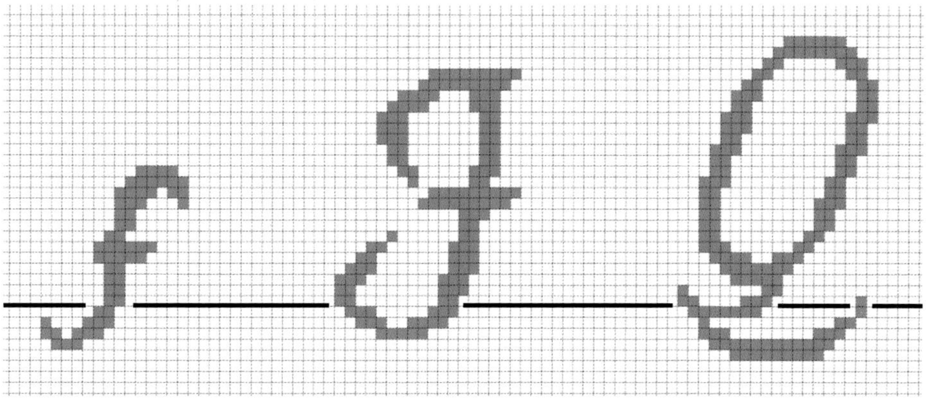

Fig. 38.

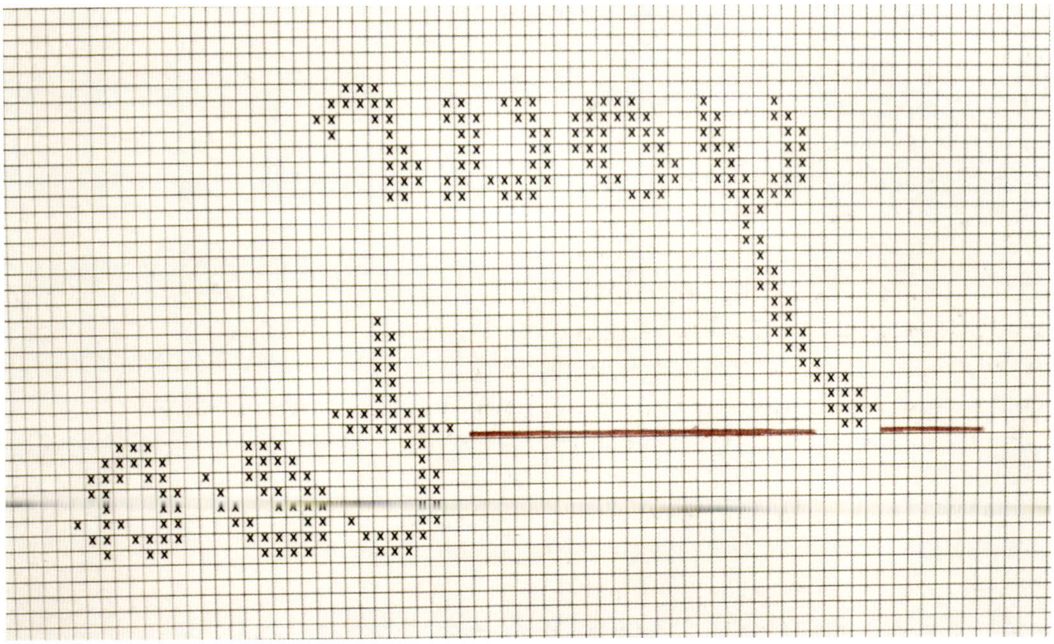

Fig. 39.
*Photo: Scott Norris*

and typically when you are distracted by other details. To avoid the mistake of overlooking a descender entirely, it is a good practice to highlight in advance the starting point of every descender in the draft, and to remind yourself often of the descenders as you weave (fig. 39).

### Letters with Bars

Several letters in the English alphabet include bars, which are the horizontal strokes seen in the uppercase *A*, *E*, *F*, *H*, and *T*, as well as some forms of *B* and *J*. Lowercase letters with bars include *f* and *t*. With these letters, the task is to avoid a long float of pattern weft at the beginning or end of the bar. This is more likely to arise in letters where one or both ends of the bar extend into open space (*E*, *F*, *J*, and *T*, and some forms of *B*, as well as the lowercase *f* and *t*), rather than the letters where the ends of the bar connect to the stems at both sides (*A*, *H*, and some forms of *B*). The issue of pattern floats can be resolved by cutting and repositioning the pattern strand, as described under "Preventing Floats in the Pattern Weft" (page 40).

### Letters with Swashes

Swashes are the expressive flourishes that decorate the apexes of some uppercase cursive and italic letters (shown in red, fig. 40).

The starting point for the swash is typically unconnected to the primary structure of the letter and generally begins at the letter's midpoint, well before your attention has turned to it. As with the letters with descenders, you can avoid the headache of a missed swash by highlighting every swash in the draft in advance.

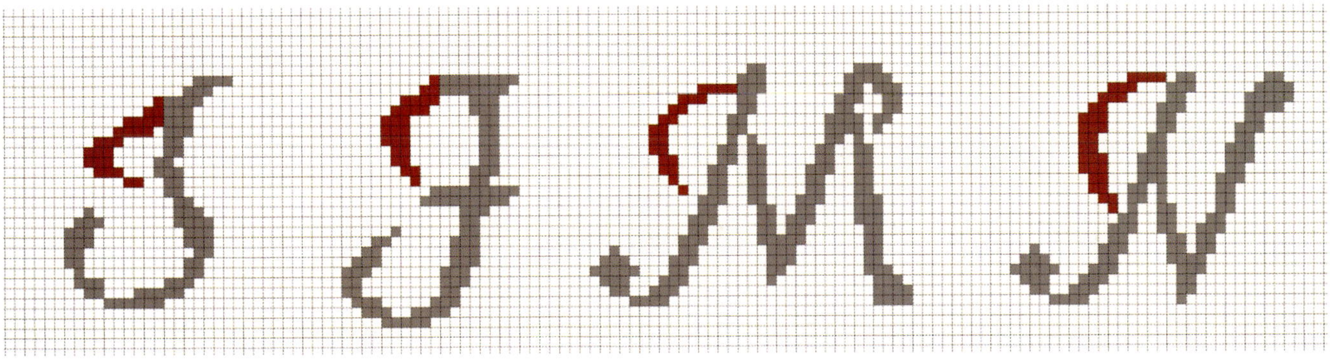

Fig. 40.

## Letters with Dots

Dotted letters such as the lowercase *i* and *j* cause few additional difficulties when laid in. To carry over the pattern strand from the body of the letter to the dot is acceptable, as long as the span does not exceed that of three raised warp ends when sett at 32 ends per inch.

## Punctuation Marks

Punctuation marks are laid in in the same manner as letters and may require special attention to ensure that they are positioned properly. For example:

The body of the comma is positioned on the same horizontal plane as the nearest letter. However, the comma's tail extends below that plane and requires the same scrutiny as letters with descenders.

The top edges of quotation marks match the imaginary horizontal line found at the height of the nearest uppercase letter. Quotation marks are typically found at a distance from the letters they accompany, and are easily overlooked. To avoid forgetting them, highlight every quotation mark in the draft.

The strand used for the dot of an exclamation mark can be carried over to the mark itself, so long as the span does not exceed that of three pattern picks at 32 picks per inch.

## Letters with Ears or Terminals

Ears can be described as the tiny swashes that are sometimes found at the top of some letters, such as the lowercase *n* and *m*. Terminals are the short tails typically seen near the base of some letters, such as the lowercase *a*. Ears and terminals may require the addition of an extra pattern strand but otherwise do not pose a particular challenge.

## Letters That Combine Angled and Vertical Lines

Many letters are made up primarily of lines that angle to the right or left, particularly in the italic and cursive scripts. Yet, even in the roman alphabets, where a large number of the characters are so-called "block" letters, numerous examples can be found that consist solely of angled lines, including *A*, *v*, *w*, and *x*.

Nevertheless, when looking at the drafts found in this book, you will see that many letters include vertical lines as well. You have options when laying in these lines, as in the choice to lay in a vertical line that "zigs" right or left. The most important consideration when laying in such letters is not whether to "zig" right or left, but to be consistent in what you do—meaning that if you decide to "zig" to the left, you should continue to make the same choice in similar situations, shed after shed, unless there is a compelling reason to do otherwise. To maintain consistency in such choices is important in fashioning an inlaid pattern that is clear and stable to the eye, rather than one that appears to drift from one option to another.

## Letters with Tight Spaces

To lay in a letter with a generous, rounded shape is one of the most pleasing aspects of weaving with words. The uppercase *B* and *D*, for example, are sunny, spacious letters. They are relatively easy to lay in. They hold your attention but allow you to relax too.

Unfortunately, other letters, while interesting in appearance, can be difficult to lay in. These letters are cramped in form and dark in color, with their various parts crowded together tightly, including the lowercase *a*, *e*, *m*, *s*, and *w* (fig. 41).

Fig. 41.

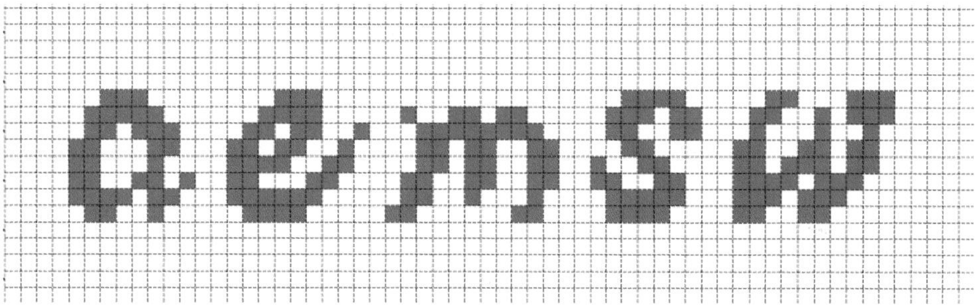

When laying in letters such as these, be careful that each part—the three legs of the lowercase *m*, for example—remain separated by at least one raised warp end without pattern in every shed. In fact, the proper placement of the pattern in a 2–4 shed is often determined solely by the need to keep different parts of a letter from touching, rather than by other criteria, such as what is attractive to the eye.

A similar concern is faced when laying in two letters that are closely spaced, side by side. In these cases, always insert the pattern strand in the 2–4 sheds so that the letters remain separated by at least one raised warp end without pattern. For more on spacing of letters and words, see chapter 2, page 59.

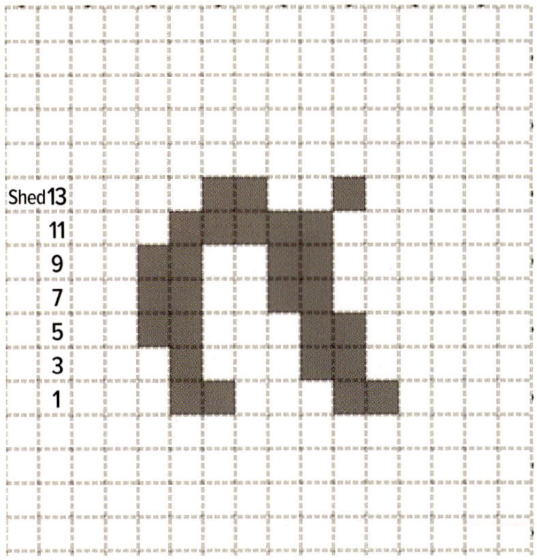


Fig. 42.

### Finishing Letters

Whenever a pattern strand is laid in within a 1–3 shed, it is assumed that a strand will be laid in within the subsequent 2–4 shed as well. However, when seeking a satisfying conclusion to some letters, it can be helpful to set these assumptions aside.

For example, I find none of the options on the left of the final 2–4 shed of the lowercase *n* to be satisfactory (fig. 42, shed 13).

On the other hand, to omit the pattern on the left from the final 2–4 shed successfully resolves the shape to my eye. Therefore, when laying in the *n*, I secure the strand at the left with a knot following shed 13 and do not lay in a strand in shed 14 (fig. 43). However, the ear at the right of the pattern is completed in the usual manner, with the strand laid in to shed 14 before being secured with a knot.

Fig. 43.

## NEXT STEPS: LAYING IN WORDS AND PHRASES

### Laying In a Word

To lay in a word is no more challenging than laying in an individual letter. However, there are many more details to think about.

The word "drink," taken from the project titled Bird Lover's Teatime on page 81, is an example of the factors to be accounted for when laying in an entire word (fig. 44). Because the process is identical to laying in a letter, and to avoid redundancy for readers already familiar with how that is done, the individual steps to lay in a word will not be described here. Instead, these guidelines focus on planning and preparation, a critical step to ensure that the letters that make up the word are spaced accurately.

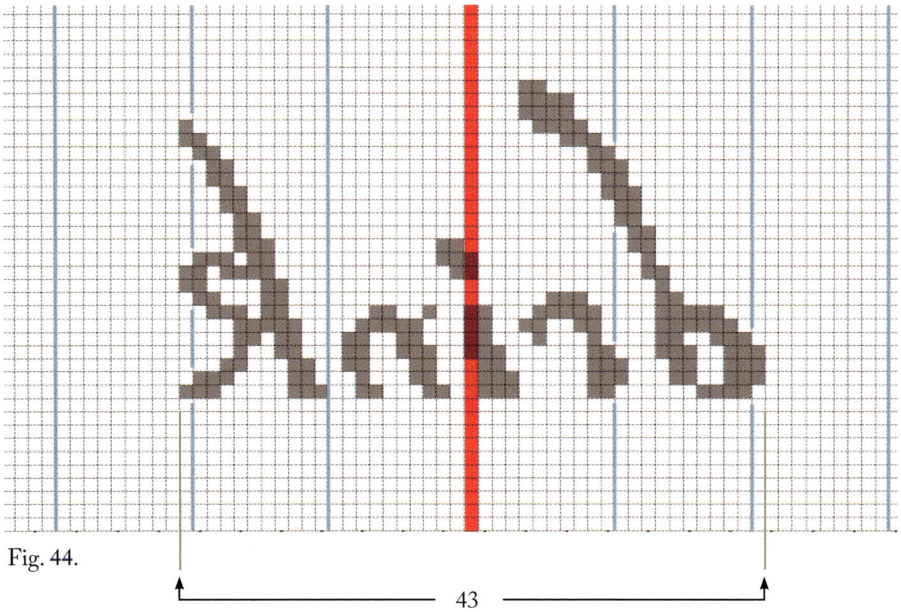

Fig. 44.

43

The center is square #22

## Guidelines for Planning and Preparation—Working to the Left

Open and hold the 1–3 shed.

Mark the raised warp end at the center. Then mark the center of the draft. Counting the squares of the first row of the draft will show you that "drink" encompasses 43 squares from left to right, with the center found in the 22nd square (indicated in red, fig 44.) For added clarity, it is also helpful to mark every 10 raised warp ends to the right and left of the center (indicated in blue).

Continuing to look at the first row of the draft, determine the number of pattern strands needed to begin laying in the word. You will see that "drink" is composed of five letters. A single strand only is needed for the letters *d*, *r*, *i*. The other letters (*n*, *k*) require two strands each.

On the basis of that tally, a total of seven pattern strands are needed to begin the pattern. Prepare those strands in advance and place them nearby. Note that both *d* and *r* will require an additional strand as the inlay process continues. While laying in, extra attention is needed to keep the various strands orderly and untangled.

Returning again to the center square of the first row, determine the exact placement of each letter (or part of a letter) to the left of center by noting the number of squares separating each letter from the center.

For example, when counting to the left you will find that the right leg of *n* occupies the second and third squares on the left; the left leg of *n* occupies the seventh and eighth squares on the left; the right leg of *k* occupies the 11th, 12th, and 13th squares on the left; and the left leg of *k* occupies the 19th, 20th, and 21st squares on the left.

In all, four pattern strands will be needed to lay in the letters *n* and *k*. Count the second and third raised warp ends to the left of center and pass the first pattern strand under those warp ends, leaving a short tail at the left. Bring the remainder of the strand upward to be carried over to the next shed. Then place the second, third, and fourth strands in the same manner, as follows:

Pass the second strand under the seventh and eighth raised warp ends on the left.

Pass the third strand under the 11th, 12th, and 13th raised warp ends on the left.

Pass the fourth strand under the 19th, 20th, and 21st raised warp ends on the left.

Doublecheck for accuracy and attach the tail of each pattern strand.

## Guidelines for Planning and Preparation—Working to the Right

Count to the right of center to prepare the placement of the three remaining strands needed to begin laying in the word. As you count, you will find that the base of *i* occupies the first, second, and third squares on the right; the base of *r* occupies the ninth and tenth squares on the right; and the base of *d* occupies the 17th through 20th squares on the right.

Therefore, pass the first strand under the first, second, and third raised warp ends to the right, leaving a tail at the left. Bring the remainder of the strand upward to be carried over. Continue to count raised warp ends to the right and place the remaining strands as follows:

Pass the second strand under the ninth and tenth raised warp ends on the right.

Pass the third strand under the 17th through 20th raised warp ends on the right.

Doublecheck for accuracy and attach the tail of each pattern strand. Throw a pick of background yarn through the same shed, beat, close the shed, and open the next shed. Subsequently, continue working upward through the draft as described in "Laying In the Lowercase *a*" until the word is complete.

## Laying In a Phrase

The process to lay in a phrase is identical to the process to lay in a word. Using the phrase "Star-of-the-meadow" (fig. 45), taken from the project of that name (chapter 3), begin by marking the center of the warp, and the center of the draft. You will see that the phrase encompasses 132 squares from left to right, with the center found at the vertical line between the 66th and 67th squares (highlighted in red, fig. 45). For clarity, mark every 10 raised warp ends to the right and left of the center (indicated in blue).

Look to the first row of the draft to determine the number of pattern strands needed to begin laying in the phrase. The phrase includes 15 letters in all, nine requiring a single strand each to begin (*S*, *t*, *r*, *o*, *f*, *t*, *e*, *e*, *o* when read from right to left). The other six letters (*a*, *h*, *m*, *a*, *d*, *w*) need two strands each. This tally shows that a total of 21 pattern strands will be needed to begin laying in the phrase. Prepare the strands in advance and place them nearby.

Be aware that as the inlay process continues, the letters *S*, *r*, *o*, *f*, *e*, *e*, and *o* will eventually require two strands each; the letters *h*, *m*, and *w* will eventually require three strands each; and three dashes will each require single strands. As a result, as many as 30 separate pattern strands will be in use at some times. Admittedly, the number of pattern strands to be kept in order and untangled may feel overwhelming. But as with every other aspect

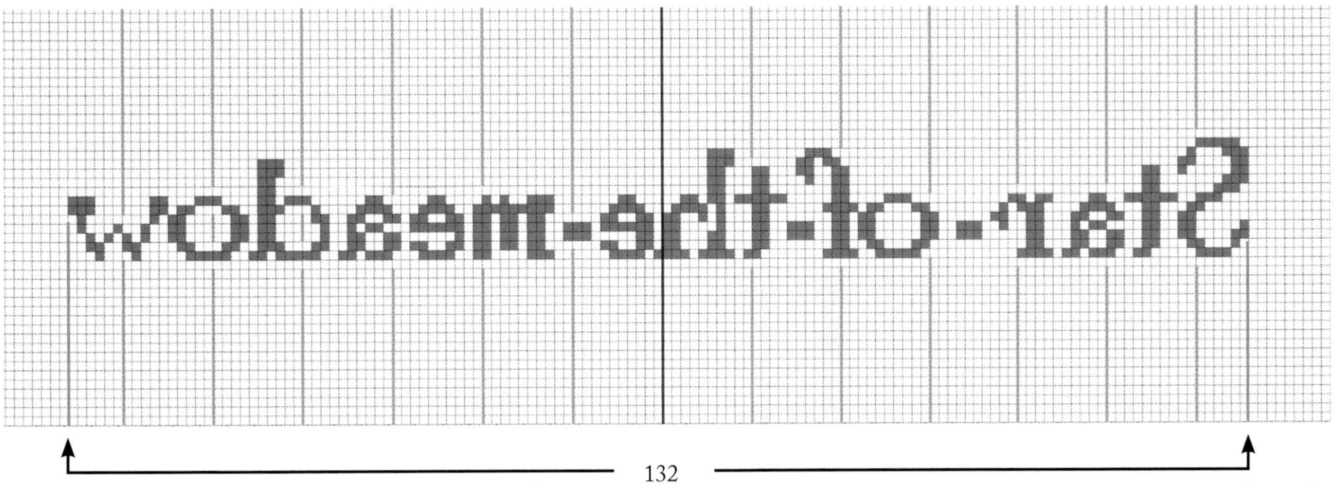


Fig. 45. The center is the line between squares #66 and #67

of woven inlay, these issues can be overcome with patience, concentration, and attention to detail. No other special skill or ability is needed.

Next, identify the placement of each letter (or part of a letter) in the first row of the draft by counting the squares to the left and right of the center. Then turn to the warp, open the 1–3 shed, and insert the pattern strands as follows:

In the draft, the left-hand leg of the letter *h* occupies four squares located almost directly at the draft's center, including the first square to the left of center, and the next three squares to the right. Accordingly, pass a pattern strand under the first raised warp end to the left of center, continuing under the next three raised warp ends to the right (four warp ends in total). Leave a tail at the left and bring the remainder of the strand upward to be carried over.

In the draft, note that the right-hand leg of *h* is located in the fifth through eighth squares to the right of center. Pass a pattern strand under the fifth raised warp end to the right of center, continuing under the next three raised warp ends to the right (four warp ends in total). Leave a tail at the left and bring the strand upward to be carried over.

In this way, you have laid in the two strands needed to begin the letter *h*. Continue working in the same manner to the right until you have inserted a total of 10 strands, including the letter *h* just completed, as well as *t*, *f*, *o*, *r*, *a*, *t*, and *S*. Note that we have begun here by working to the right rather than the left, simply because the letter *h*, which is located nearest the center, falls to the right side of the draft.

Double-check for accuracy. Then repeat the same process to the left, beginning with the letter *e* and continuing letter by letter until reaching *w*. In all, you will insert 11 pattern strands to the left of center. When combined with those inserted to the right, you will have laid in a total of 21 strands.

Securely attach each tail, throw a pick of background yarn through the same shed, beat, close the shed, and open the next shed. Then continue working upward through the draft as described in "Laying In the Lowercase *a*."

## OTHER CONSIDERATIONS

Other considerations will engage your mind as you plan and carry out an inlay project—including the number of ends per inch in the warp, what fibers to use, how hard to beat, and how to solve problems when they arise.

### Sett

As with overshot, the pattern weft for inlay requires extra space for close beating. For this reason, inlay is woven using a sett that is more open in texture than is usual for plain weave without inlay. For example, 40/2 linen is often sett at approximately 36 ends per inch (e.p.i.) for plain weave. However, setts of 28–32 e.p.i. are more appropriate when 40/2 linen is used for inlay.

Cloth with extensive inlay generally calls for a more open sett than cloth with less inlay. This factor accounts for the range of setts in the examples given above, with cloth woven from 40/2 linen that contains a large amount of inlay typically sett at 28 e.p.i., cloth with a moderate amount of inlay sett at 30 e.p.i., and cloth with a limited amount of inlay sett at 32 e.p.i.

### The Weight of the Pattern Weft

Inlaid patterns are clearer in appearance when laid in with a pattern weft that is heavier than the background. Using a pattern weft that is approximately twice the weight of the background is a good starting point. But it is important to select a weight of yarn that does not prevent you from beating each weft pick firmly into place. Patterns laid in using yarn that is too heavy will become elongated in shape, with circles stretched into ovals, and squares into rectangles. Conversely, patterns laid in with a weft that is too light will appear compressed in shape.

In some cases, replacing a pattern weft with the next graded weight, such as 20/2 linen replaced by 30/2 linen, will quickly bring the pattern into balance. In other cases, an element of improvisation is required to achieve a balanced pattern. For example, when laying in patterns on a background of 40/2 linen sett at 32 ends per inch, it is often effective to insert a doubled strand of 40/2 linen

into each 1–3 shed, and a single strand of 40/2 linen into each 2–4 shed, while maintaining that doubled strand–single strand alternation consistently throughout (fig. 46).

Fig. 46.

Other options for correcting an unbalanced pattern include sleying at a more open sett, or relaxing the tension on the warp to allow close beating. These strategies are also helpful to address the "buildup" of the pattern weft that can occur when weaving areas that are densely filled with pattern.

### Beating Inlaid Patterns

Many factors influence the amount of pressure needed to beat a laid-in pattern.

Little pressure is needed if you're working with fine yarn or weaving cloth of a relaxed, open texture, such as 60/2 linen sett at 24 ends per inch. Considerably more pressure is needed when weaving with heavier yarn, when that yarn is sett more closely, or when a dense, tightly woven texture is desired, such as that typically sought for dish towels and other household textiles.

In addition, the degree of pressure while beating will vary depending on the nature of the inlaid pattern being woven. Patterns consisting solely of slender lines call for only slightly firmer beating, while patterns with more-extensive inlay will require considerably firmer beating in order to "square" the pattern. (See "Inlaid Patterns That Draw In"below.)

An added difficulty is to beat consistently when laying in a pattern with varying amounts of inlay, such as when narrow, inlaid lines gradually converge as densely inlaid areas. In these cases, you should often check the number of background picks woven per inch (not background picks *plus* pattern picks), with the goal to achieve a texture that is consistently as nearly square as possible, despite the variation in the density of the inlaid pattern. When weaving a pattern with an extensive amount of inlay, it is unlikely that you will produce a texture that is perfectly square, particularly when weaving on a wider warp. For example, when weaving a dense area of inlay on a warp sett at 32 ends per inch, and a warp that is 18 to 24 inches in width, I typically achieve 28–30 background picks per inch. On the other hand, I usually reach 32 picks per inch when weaving a closely worked pattern on a warp that is 5 inches in width or less.

Consistency in beating rather than perfection is the goal. If you are beating 30 picks per inch while weaving the densely filled sections of an inlaid pattern, you should try to maintain 30 picks per inch in the more sparsely filled sections as well. Frequent use of a tape measure or ruler to count the number of weft picks per inch is helpful to maintain consistent beating.

### Inlaid Patterns That Draw In

Inlaid patterns tighten or "draw in" under the pressure of beating, just as any weft pick will draw in as the cloth is beaten. In the worst cases, drawing in can cause unsightly gaps at the edges of a laid-in pattern. Items with extensive areas of inlay will often draw in more than items with less inlay, due to the greater pressure required to beat square. The problem can be eliminated by leaving each pattern strand lying loosely in the shed, allowing small loops to appear at the edge of the pattern, and avoiding the temptation to pull the strand tight in order to make it neat in appearance.

### Working with Pattern Strands

In general, 4 to 6 inches is a good length for a pattern strand. There are benefits to using longer strands, because they reduce the frequency at which depleted strands must be replaced (see "Durability" below). Strands that are 10 to 12 inches in length are useful when filling wide areas of a pattern, as seen in some of the projects found in chapter 3. However, long strands can be unwieldy. Some weavers might find it helpful to wrap longer strands as "butterflies." For

LEFT: *The months ahead*, 48" × 79", linen, 2021, detail

me, butterflies add extra steps to the process without making it significantly easier, and I'm happiest when working with relatively short strands that I allow to dangle freely, separating them carefully as I work. A pair of 5-inch forceps can be helpful for untangling one pattern strand from the rest.

Another challenge is the awkwardness of passing a pattern strand across a wide distance in an open shed. Again, a butterfly might be the answer, or using a crochet or sley hook to pass the strand through the shed. Clumsy as I am, I find that my fingers alone are the quickest, easiest solution.

### Yarns and Fibers

Depending on the effect that is desired, yarns of any fiber are suitable for inlay, including wool, silk, cotton, and linen. In terms of both background and pattern, finer yarns that are evenly and firmly spun will allow the weaver to create subtle shapes and gradually curving lines without the visible "sawtooth" seen when using heavier yarns. To form more complicated shapes such as letters and words typically calls for relatively fine yarns, such as linen graded at 40/2 or less.

However, heavy, irregular, or loosely spun yarns can be effective for inlay as well, particularly when a "textural" effect is desired. Mixed-fiber inlay is possible, such a wool pattern laid in to a cotton or linen background. In these cases, samples should be woven and washed before beginning a project, so that differences in shrinkage and other factors can be accounted for.

### Preventing Floats in the Pattern Weft

Consistency while weaving is advantageous for many reasons. Long-standing habits save time because, by relying on the "body memory" that develops from repetitive physical actions, we repeat certain movements without taking time to think about what we're doing. Being consistent also reduces the possibility of error, because we become skilled in practices that we repeat often and are more likely to do them correctly.

With consistency in mind, it is a good practice to pass the pattern strands and background wefts from left to right in the 1–3 sheds, and right to left in the 2–4 sheds. However, in some instances, to strictly maintain this practice would require you to pass a strand over an unacceptably wide span. In such cases, the long pattern float can be avoided in one of two ways:

Cut and secure the pattern strand laid in to the previous shed with a knot or loop. Then lay in a new strand in the next shed in a position that eliminates the float. Maintain the standard left-to-right (1–3 sheds) and right-to-left (2–4 sheds) ordering of the strands.

Or, reverse the left-to-right, right-to-left ordering of the pattern strand temporarily whenever that reversal allows the strand to be laid in without a long float. Continue laying in the strand in the reversed order until the next convenient opportunity to restore the original order.

### Durability

The durability of an inlaid pattern is important for items intended for everyday use and regular washing, such as dish towels or napkins. In general, durability increases when fewer, longer strands are used, and when the beginning and end of each strand is knotted securely with a simple overhand knot to the nearest raised warp end. When tightly woven from good-quality cotton or linen, such items can be machine washed on a cold-water setting.

Durability is less important for items that are not intended for daily use. For these items, including framed wall pieces or decorative pillows, a pattern strand can be secured by looping the tail of the strand around the nearest raised warp end at both the beginning and end, passing the tail under the two closest raised warp ends in the open shed, before bringing it upward through the raised warp. If washing is necessary, such pieces should be washed by hand only.

### Broken Warp Ends

You may experience an increase in broken warps ends when weaving inlay, typically within an inch or two of the selvages. This breakage results from the added strain on the warp caused by holding the shed open for long periods of time while laying

**ABOVE:**
*Hens*, 18" × 30", linen, 2024, detail

in the pattern. Various techniques can be used to reduce such breakage, including the following:

Advancing the warp often will keep the "fell of the cloth" nearer to the breast beam, resulting in a more relaxed shed that puts less strain on the selvages.

If the appearance of a selvage is not important to you—such as when it will be hidden by a seam after it is joined to another piece of cloth, or if you follow other criteria to assess quality—the strain on the selvages can be reduced by leaving short, ⅛-inch loops of background weft with every pick. Such loops reduce the draw-in that causes broken warp ends at the selvages.

When weaving with linen, broken warp ends can be reduced by lightly dampening the warp with water (an ordinary spray bottle with a nozzle and trigger works well for this purpose). Adding water to the warp can cause other problems, such as discoloration of the linen itself, or rusting of loom parts made from iron or steel. However, if such problems are not a concern, the dampening of a linen warp is an effective way to eliminate broken warp ends almost entirely.

### Carrying Over

To carry over a pattern strand from one shed to the next is a valuable time-saver, and, when laying in on the back of the cloth, the carryover is invisible when the cloth is seen from the front. However, the floats of pattern weft that can result when carrying over a wide distance are vulnerable to snagging. When working with relatively fine yarns such as 40/2 linen (28–32 e.p.i.), it is a good rule to carry over a span of no more than three raised warp ends at any one time. That number should be reduced when weaving with heavier yarns or more-open setts. If the distance is too wide, the pattern strand should be cut and secured with a knot or loop when completing the previous shed, and a new strand inserted in the next shed.

### Making Mistakes, Avoiding Mistakes

Mistakes are a fact of life for every weaver and, if minor, are often of little concern. However, inlaid patterns grow cumulatively, with the pattern in one shed placed according to the position of the pattern in the previous shed. For this reason, even a minor inaccuracy can quickly lead to a distorted pattern.

Despite good intentions, it is nearly impossible to avoid mistakes completely. In a perfect world, the number of random, unforeseen, and frustrating mistakes that any weaver of inlay might make will be reduced significantly by working in an unhurried, patient manner, while blocking out any outside distractions.

But for those of us living in the endlessly distracting real world, a few strategies for preventing errors can be useful. For me, the most common errors are made when counting raised warp ends, leading to patterns that are misshaped or that are positioned incorrectly in the warp. To check for accuracy in these situations, always count again the number of raised warp ends under which any pattern strand has been inserted, and check that count against the draft. When weaving a complex pattern, with multiple strands inserted at different points into each shed, count the number of raised warp ends without pattern that separate each strand from the next, and check that count against the draft. In my experience, to follow these practices consistently eliminates these mistakes.

Another common error is to accidentally skip a shed, instead moving on to lay in the pattern in the next row of the draft. This mistake can be avoided by carefully marking each row of the draft as soon as it is completed. In my case, I must be absolutely strict about marking the draft with a horizontal pencil line immediately after completing each row. If I do anything in the meantime—such as changing the bobbin used for the background—I will inevitably forget to make the mark, typically with disastrous results. Yes, a heavily marked draft can be a mess to look at, but I'm happy to trade an appearance of disarray for a pattern that has been laid in without mistakes (fig. 47).

### Washing and Finishing

Prior to washing and finishing, the various tails that remain on the back of the cloth can be trimmed. Tails that have been secured with knots can be trimmed to ⅛ inch. Tails that have been secured by looping can be trimmed to ½ inch.

Fig. 47.

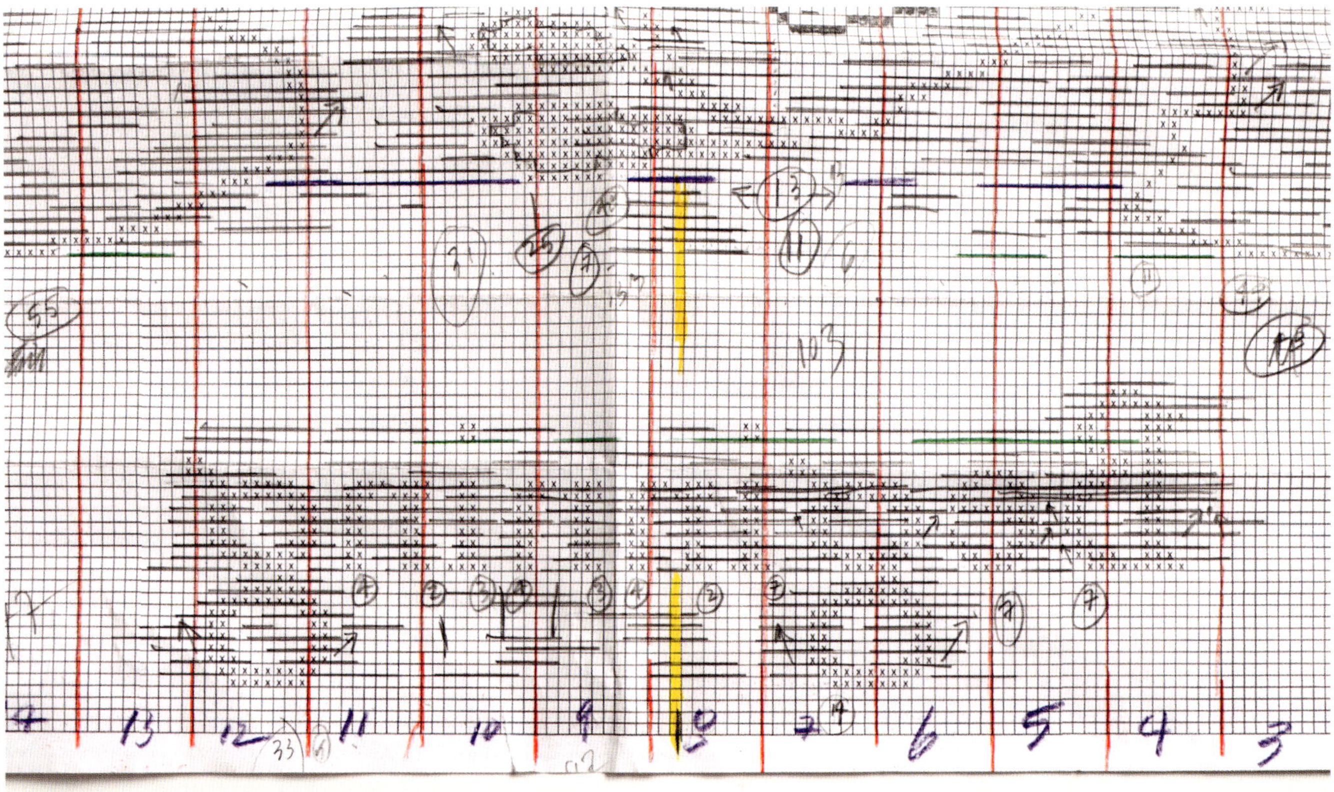

As noted under "Durability," items that are tightly woven from good-quality cotton or linen can be machine washed in cold water, provided that every pattern strand has been securely knotted to the warp. Such items should be line-dried or dried flat and should be steam-ironed on the front of the cloth, at the highest setting recommended for the fiber.

Items in which the pattern strands have been attached to the warp by looping rather than knotting, or items with an open, gauze-like, or otherwise delicate texture should be hand-washed in cold water and dried flat. Such items can be lightly ironed on the front of the cloth, if ironing is recommended for the fiber.

### Laying In Patterns with Color

The use of color can add immeasurably to the appeal of an inlaid pattern. Color can be used to highlight a shape by outlining it with inlaid lines, or a shape can be filled completely with a single color. A combination of these two approaches can be used as well. For instance, the diver portrayed in the project titled Neptune in chapter 3 is depicted entirely by outlining in blue. Most of the flowers shown in the Star-of-the-Meadow placemat project have petals and leaves that are filled completely with single colors. Yet, that project also includes yellow flowers with pink borders, showing a combination of outlining and filling.

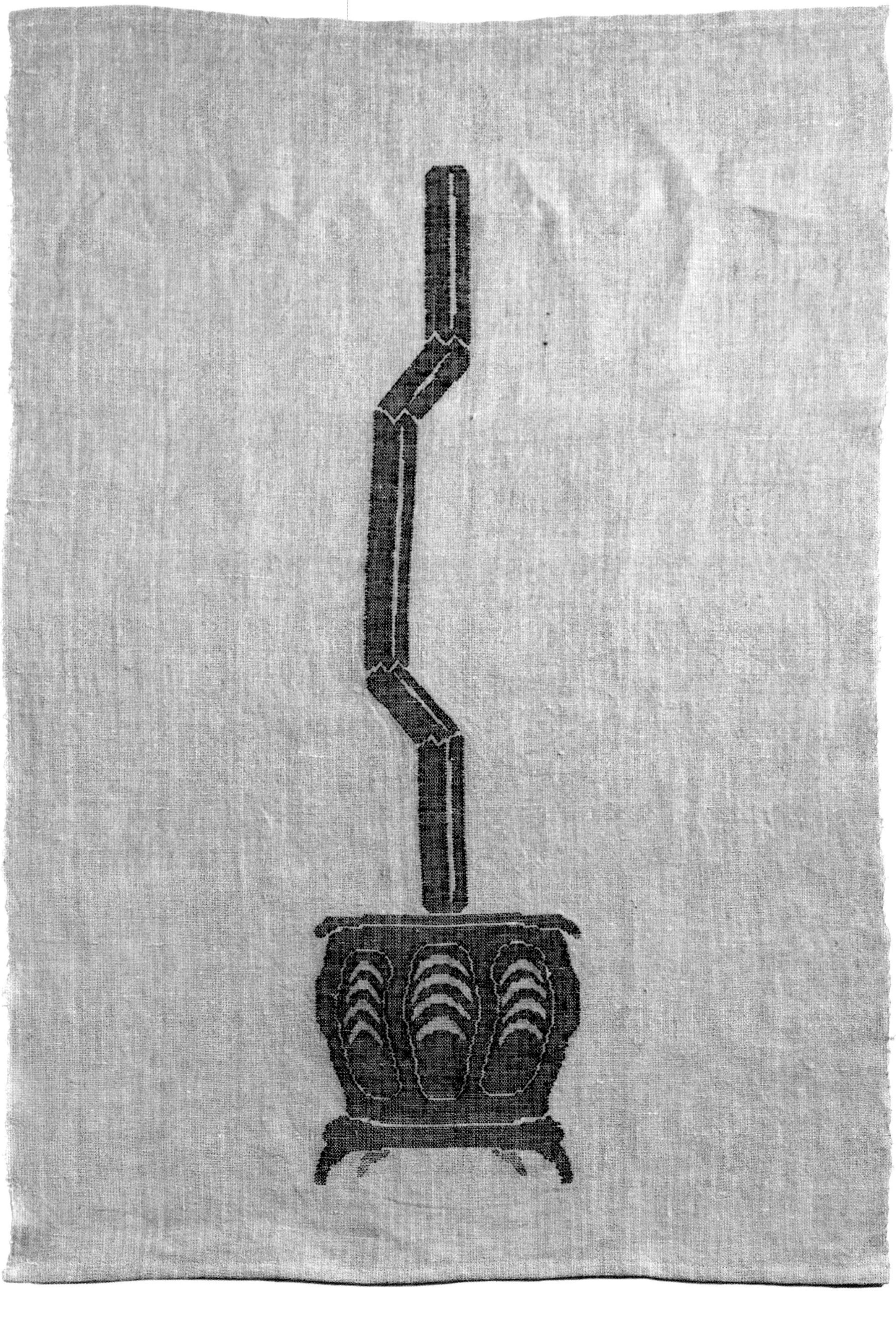

## — *Chapter 2* —

# DRAFTING

There are many ways to draft patterns for woven inlay. Drafting freehand, while spontaneously creating the shapes seen in your mind's eye, can be invaluable. However, there are benefits to a methodical, step-by-step approach to design—particularly for weavers who, like me, do not think of themselves as designers or artists.

First, a step-by-step approach encourages you to pay close attention to every facet of the design, and that is helpful to understand what makes a successful pattern. Second, a more considered approach saves time by limiting the mistakes that come with spontaneity, as well as the number of samples that are woven while correcting those mistakes. Third, a methodical approach promotes a welcome element of predictability, consistency, and regularity. Over time, you will discover effects that please you, and you can develop and repeat "formulas" to produce the same effects again.

Lines that seem to have been drawn with the freedom of a pencil on paper are essential when drafting for inlay. These *design elements* move at different angles, reverse direction, and curve. They are the foundation for almost every design style imaginable.

### DESIGN ELEMENT: AN ANGLED LINE AT 45°

To draft a line angling to the right at 45°, begin by filling (or marking with an X or other symbol) a single square in the bottom row of a graph. In the next row above, fill a second square, shifting one column to the right. (In this context, "column" refers to the squares when viewed vertically.) Continue this process, working upward row by row, until the line reaches the length you have planned (fig. 1). Keep in mind that a variety of factors, such as the sett, the pressure exerted while beating, and the thickness of the background yarn or pattern weft, can lead to variations in the degree of angle of a laid-in line. Sample first to ensure that you obtain the degree of angle that you have planned.

To draft a line that angles to the left at 45°, shift one column to the left with every row.

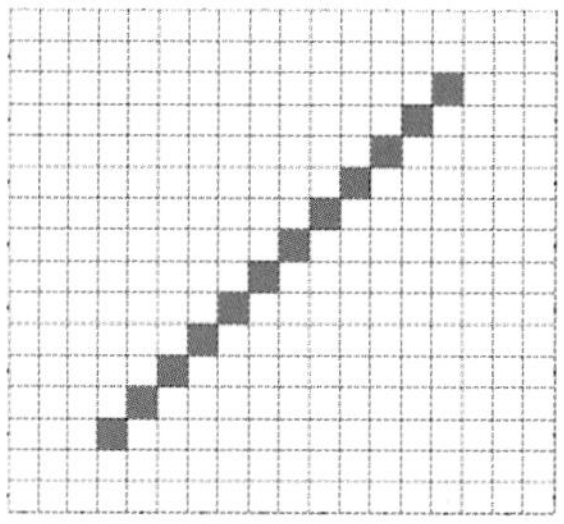

Fig. 1.

### DESIGN ELEMENT: AN ANGLED LINE AT 60°

To draft a line angling to the right at 60°, begin by filling two squares in the first and second rows of a graph, one square directly above the other. Move upward to the third and fourth rows of the graph and continue by filling two additional squares, one directly above the other, shifting one column to the right. Repeat this process, working upward two rows at a time, inserting two filled squares one above the other with each upward step, shifting one column to the right each time, until the line reaches the length you want (fig. 2).

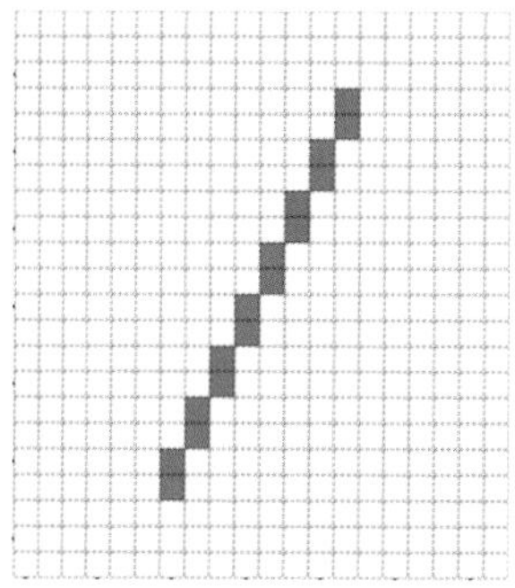

Fig. 2.

OPPOSITE:

*Potbellied stove*,
18" × 28", linen, 2023

To draft a line that angles to the left at 60°, shift one column to the left with every two rows.

## DESIGN ELEMENT: ANGLED LINES OF HIGH DEGREE (70°, 75°, 80°, 85°)

When following the process just described, the degree of angle of a line *increases* as the number filled squares *increases*. For example:

Three filled squares inserted one above the other will make a line that angles at 70° (fig. 3a).

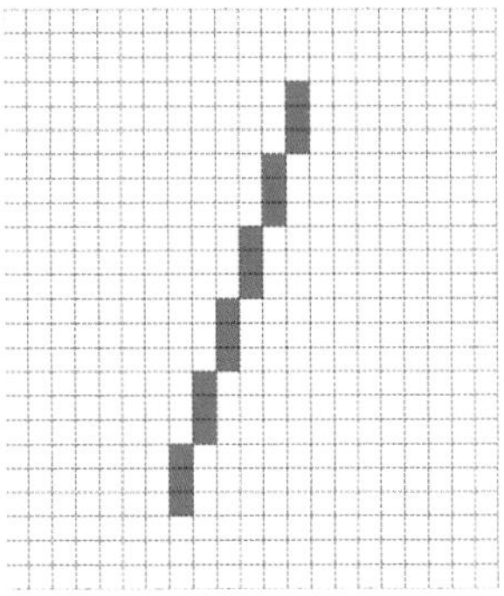

Fig. 3a.

Four filled squares inserted one above the other will make a line that angles at 75° (fig. 3b).

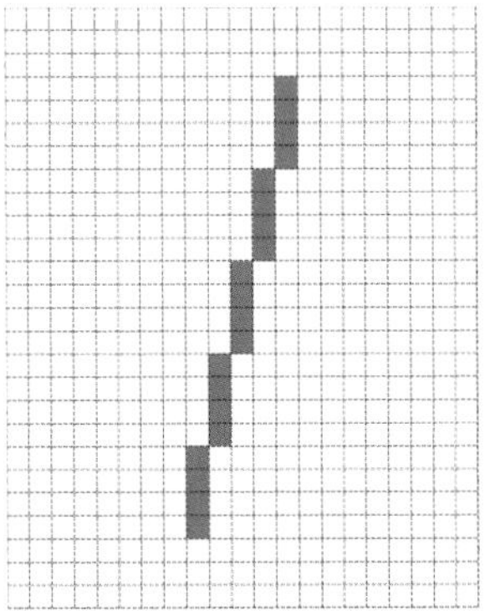

Fig. 3b.

By continuing in this manner, a line that angles at 80° is formed when six filled squares are inserted one above the other, and a line that angles at 85° is formed when eight filled squares are inserted one above the other. As before, the same steps can be followed to draft lines that angle to the right or left.

## DESIGN ELEMENT: ANGLED LINES OF LOW DEGREE (5°)

To draft a line angling to the right at 5°, begin by inserting eight filled squares side by side in a single row at the bottom of a graph. In the next row above, insert a second group of eight filled squares, positioned directly to the right of the first group. Continue to work upward row by row, until the line reaches the length you have planned. In each row, insert another group of eight filled squares, directly to the right of the group in the previous row (fig. 4).

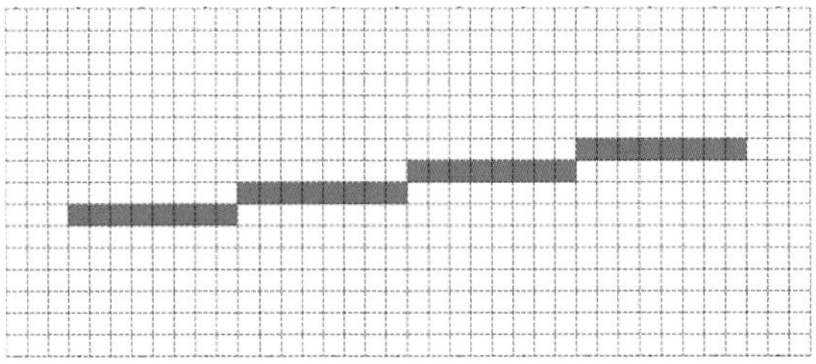

Fig. 4.

## DESIGN ELEMENT: ADDITIONAL LINES OF LOW DEGREE (10°, 15°, 20°, 30°)

When following the process just described, the degree of angle of a line of low degree *increases* as the length of each group *decreases*. For example,

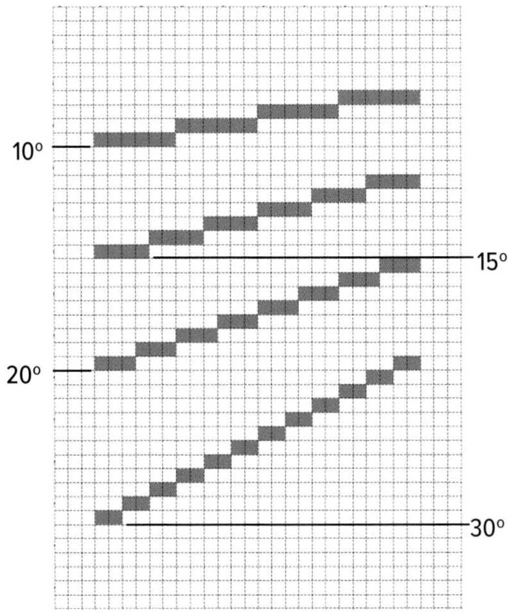


Fig. 5.

groups consisting of six filled squares per row will make a line that angles at 10°, groups consisting of four filled squares per row will make a line that angles at 15°, groups consisting of three filled squares per row will make a line that angles at 20°, and groups consisting of two filled squares per row will make a line that angles at 30° (fig. 5). The same steps can be followed to draft lines that angle to the right or left.

## DESIGN ELEMENT: CURVING LINES

The previous sections provided techniques for drafting simple lines—that is, angled lines that do not change direction. The next step is to draft lines that curve.

A reliable way to draft a curve is to base it on a predetermined angle. First, determine the height and width of the curve, and the degree of angle to be used. In fig. 6a, the curve is 27 rows high and 14 columns wide, and the degree of angle is 45°. With those decisions having been made, begin by marking the starting point, midpoint, and end point of the curve you're planning. Whether the starting point is the top or bottom does not matter. Note that the height of the curve shown here is approximately twice its width, a characteristic of curves based on a 45° angle.

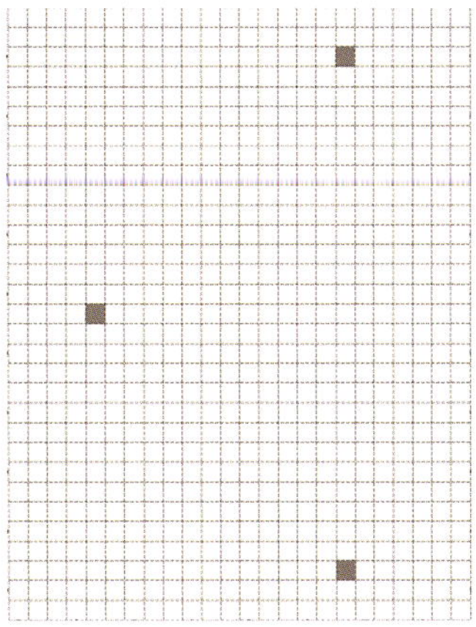

Fig. 6a.

Subsequently, follow the steps in Design element: An angled line at 45° to insert pairs of filled squares to make an angled line at 45°, connecting the starting point at the bottom of the graph to the midpoint. Then work upward from the midpoint to the end point in the same manner, reversing the direction of the angle to fashion a second angled line at 45°. You will create a thin angled line that resembles a person's arm when bent at the elbow, with each half of the angled line consisting of 14 pairs of filled squares, and with the pair at the elbow counted as part of each angled line (fig. 6b).

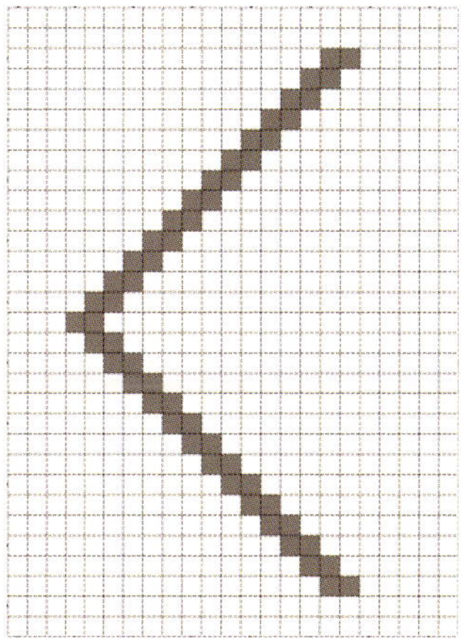

Fig. 6b.

Continue to refine this "arm" by inserting filled squares into the shallow space inside the elbow, as shown in red (fig. 6c), which begins to obscure the sharply defined lines of the underlying 45° angle.

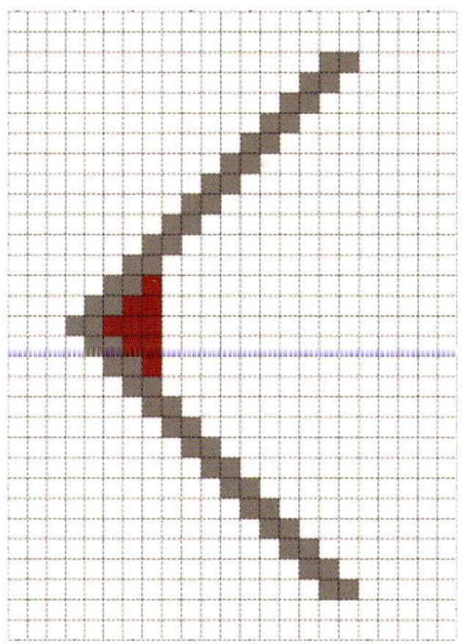

Fig. 6c.

Then work upward from the elbow, inserting additional filled squares at the outside of the shape as shown in red (fig. 6d). Just above the elbow, insert only one or two filled squares per row. Midway between the elbow and shoulder, add extra filled squares to make a shape that swells outward when compared to the more thinly shaped elbow. As you approach the shoulder, reduce the number of filled squares to roughly match the rows above the elbow.

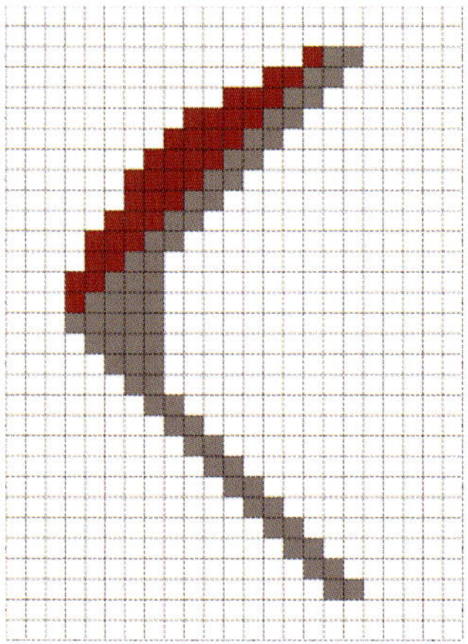

Fig. 6d.

Repeat the same process below the elbow, forming an exact, mirror image of the additions you made above the elbow (fig. 6e).

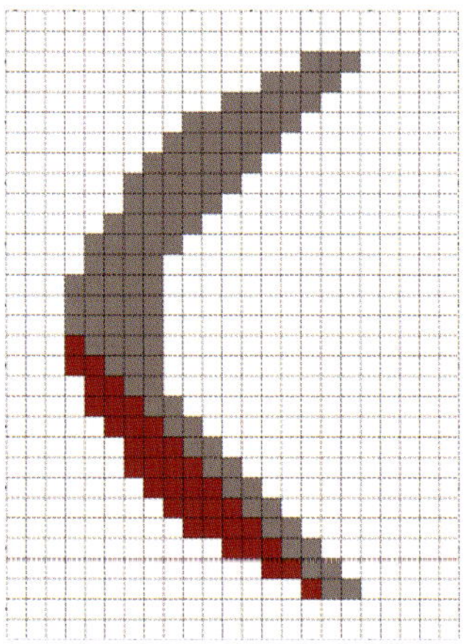

Fig. 6e.

Note that as currently drawn, the two angled lines that form this curve merely point up and down

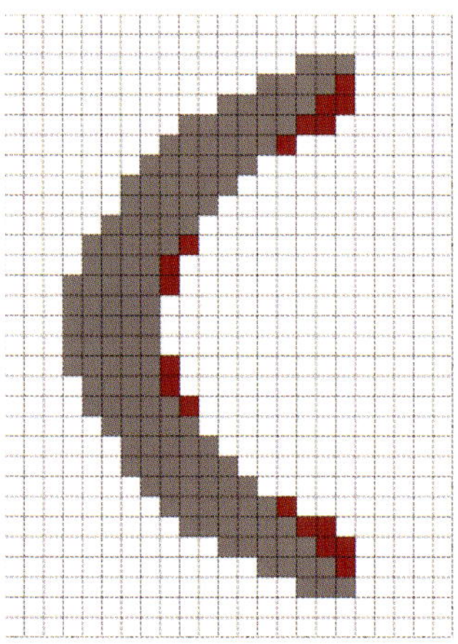

Fig. 6f.

and lack a decisive movement to the right, while the hard lines of the original 45° angle are still somewhat visible at the inside of the shape. Adding a few additional filled squares softens the angle on the inside, while also helping to make a curve that turns more emphatically to the right (fig. 6f).

## DESIGN ELEMENT: VARIABLE CURVING LINES

In contrast to the previous curve, the angle of a curve can be varied freely to achieve different effects. For example, when followed from the bottom to the top, the curve shown in fig. 7a begins at an angle of 10° before transitioning upward through 20°, 30°, 45°, 60°, and 75°. This curve is almost horizontal at its beginning, and nearly vertical when it ends. It is what might be called a "variable curving line"—that is, a line that changes degree at different points. An algorithm could be created from this curve, such as *Two rows at 10° followed by three rows at 20° followed by three rows at 30° followed by three rows at 45° followed by four columns at 60° followed by four columns at 75°.*

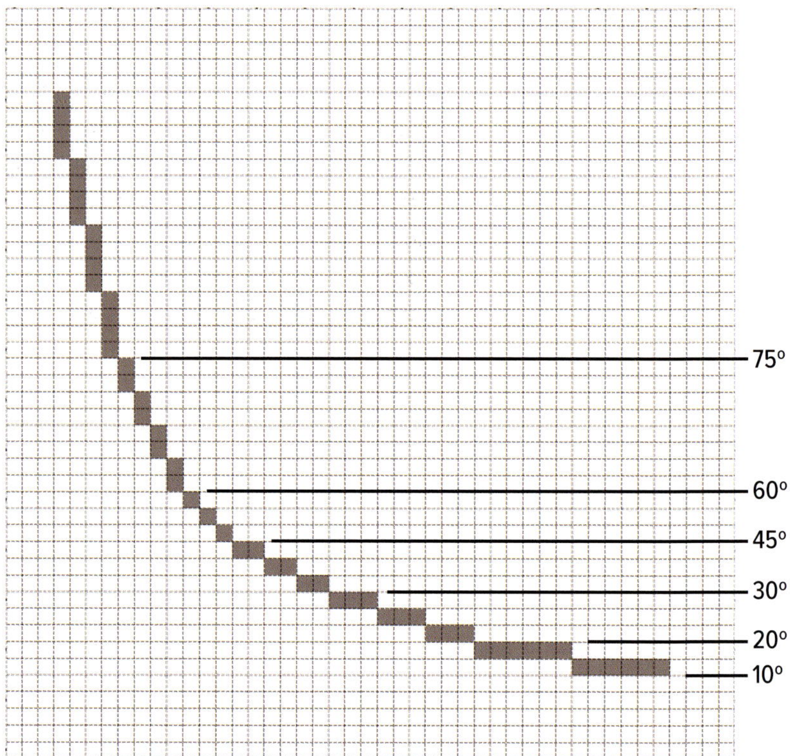


Fig. 7a.

Fig. 7b.

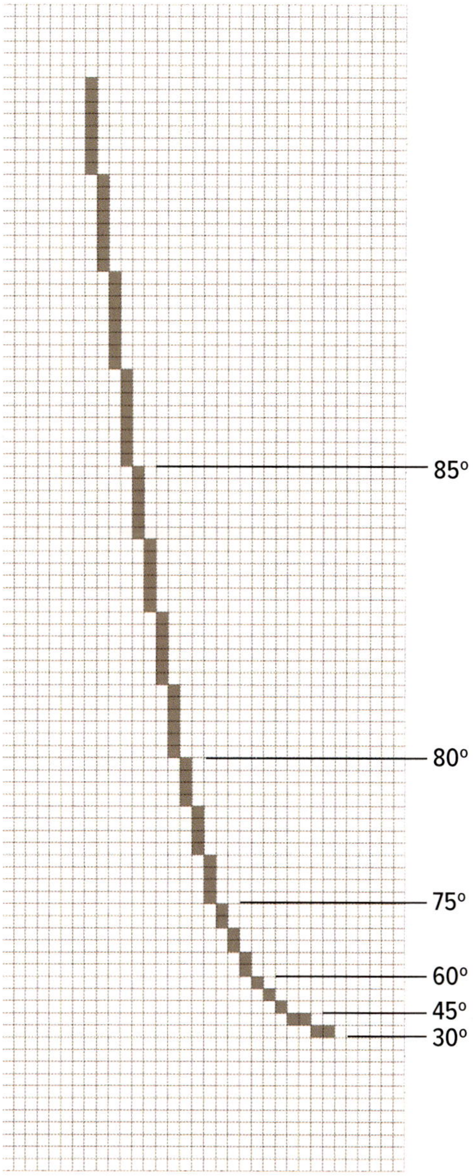


To repeat this algorithm by using higher degrees of angle would produce a curve that ascends more steeply upward, and with less horizontal movement (fig. 7b), such as *Two rows at 30° followed by three rows at 45° followed by three columns at 60° followed by three columns at 75° followed by four columns at 80° followed by four columns at 85°.*

Conversely, to follow this algorithm by using lower degrees of angle would produce a curve that ascends more slowly, with a greater percentage of its motion being to the side (fig. 7c). For example, *Two rows at 5° followed by three rows at 10° followed by three rows at 20° followed by three rows at 30° followed by four rows at 45° followed by four columns at 60°.*

An endless number of different curves can be developed, and a curve can be created without relying on an algorithm. The curves and algorithms given here merely furnish a framework for planning a variable curving line that passes through different degrees of angle. However, keeping a small library of algorithms will allow you to repeat a curve at a later time without having to plot it again.

Fig. 7c.

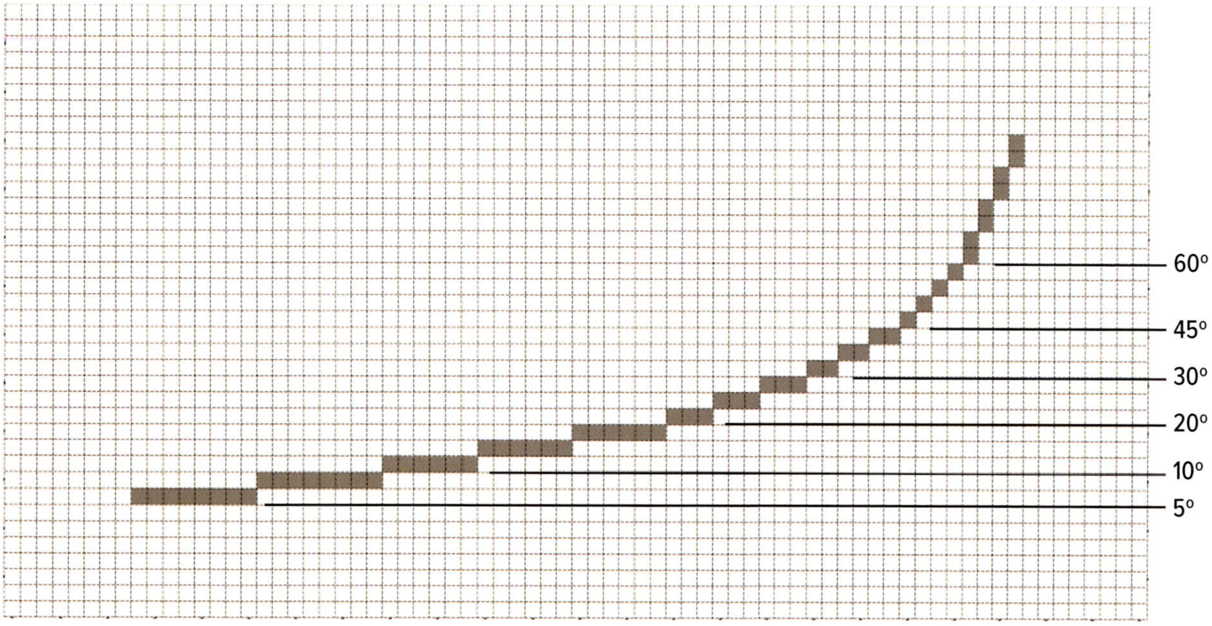

# DESIGN ELEMENT: VARIABLE CURVING LINES IN CURSIVE AND ITALIC ALPHABETS

Variable curving lines are common in cursive handwriting, as well as the italic forms of the English alphabet. For example, the leading edge of the ascender of the letter *b* shown in fig. 8a is a variable curving line that transitions through three different degrees, including six rows at 90°, six rows at 60°, and five rows at 45°.

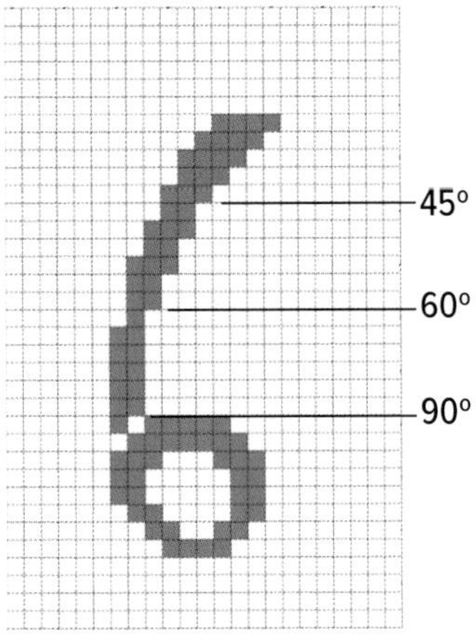


Fig. 8a.

On the other hand, the leading edge of the ascender of the letter *h* shown in fig. 8b demonstrates a simpler profile, transitioning between two degrees only, including eight rows at 60° and nine rows at 45°. It is a more gradual and relaxed curve.

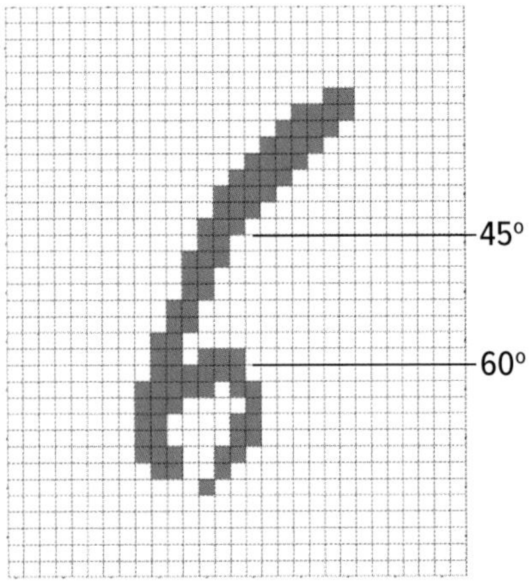


Fig. 8b.

A very different shape is provided by the letter *t* shown in fig. 8c. It is short and squat, with a hook-shaped curve that shifts quickly from 45° to 90° to 45° below the bar, and from 45° to 60° above it. The letter has a tight, energetic shape, as if it resulted from a fast stroke of the pen.

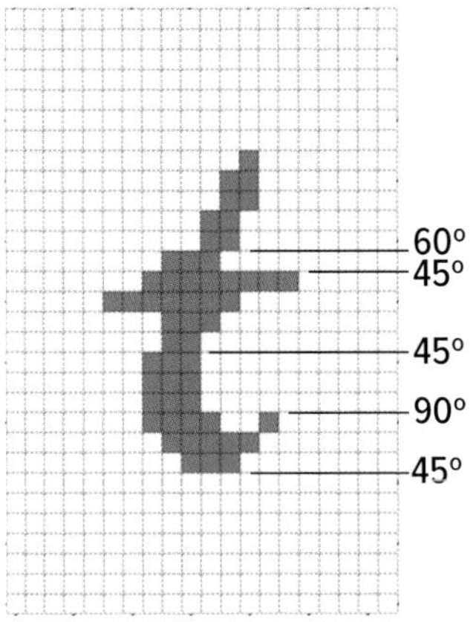


Fig. 8c.

As with ascenders, a variety of angles are often found in descenders. For example, the descender of the lowercase *g* shown in fig. 8d consists of two variable curving lines that slope to the right in parallel. While parallel, the two lines shift in degree somewhat independently of one another, with one line sometimes turning upward while the other turns to the right, and so on. As a result, the overall shape of the descender is flexible, broadening at the bottom and narrowing at the top, moving gracefully and casually.

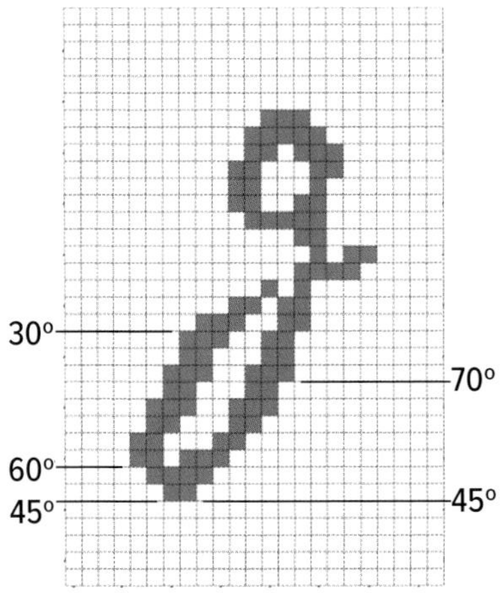


Fig. 8d.

## DRAFTING DEMONSTRATION: VARIABLE CURVING LINES IN ACTION

Beyond cursive and italic scripts, variable curving lines are found in numerous other pattern shapes. Given the freedom of curving lines, it can be helpful to organize them around an underlying structure, such as a predetermined angle or an algorithm as just described, or a geometric shape. In this approach, squares and rectangles are particularly useful. They add a reliable framework that allows you to test a pattern's proportions in advance—if the size and arrangement of the squares and rectangles look right to you, you can expect the proportions of the finished design to look right as well. Basing your design on geometric shapes lends a solid underpinning to the resulting pattern, ensuring that it is organized around fixed points and planes, while bringing focus and clarity to the design—such as that of an ordinary pottery cup.

### Preparation

First, decide on the dimensions of the cup you have in mind, and draft a square or rectangle that encompasses the height and width of the cup you have imagined.

For instance, to draft a broad, stocky cup, begin with a rectangle that is 50 columns wide and 25 rows high. Mark the center with a vertical line (fig. 9a).

Next, assuming that you will be seeing this cup slightly from above, draft a second rectangle that represents the dimensions of the opening of the cup, positioned directly above the first. Arrange the rectangle symmetrically so that its bottom line is located five rows below the upper line of the first rectangle, while its top line is five rows

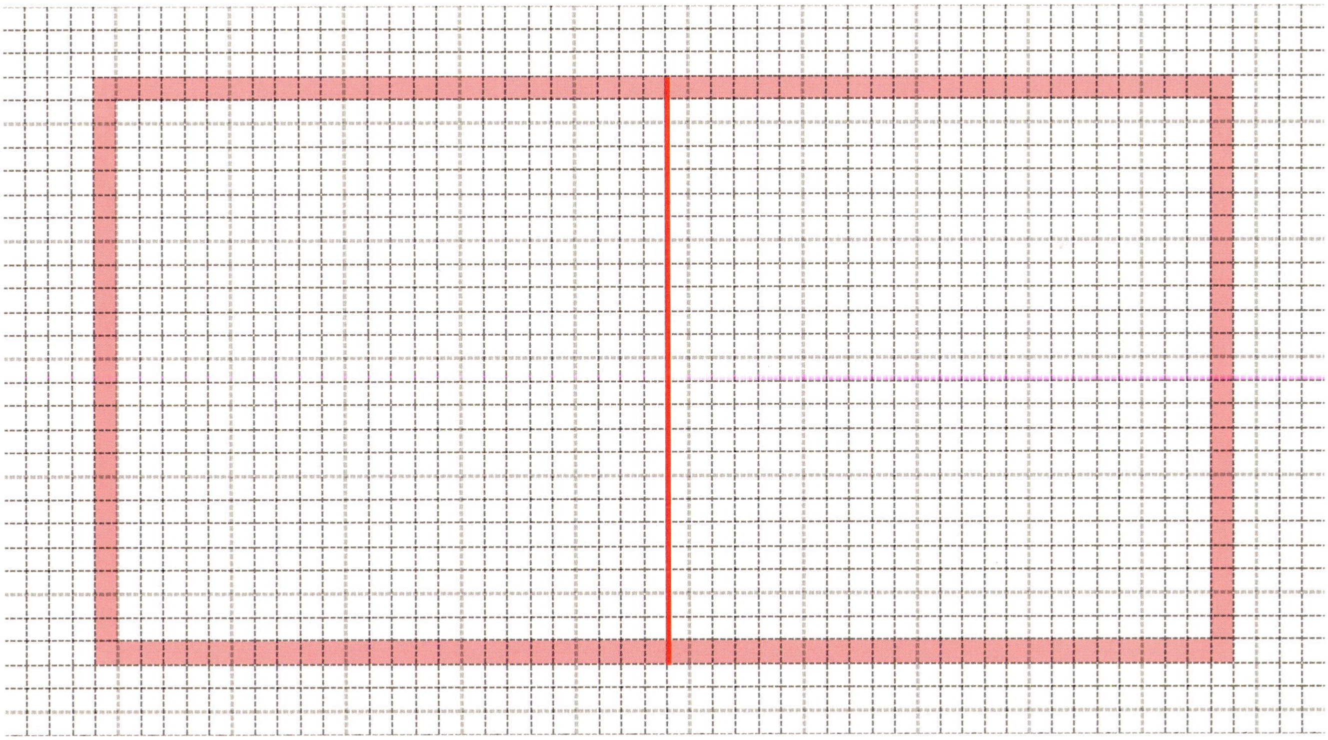

Fig. 9a.

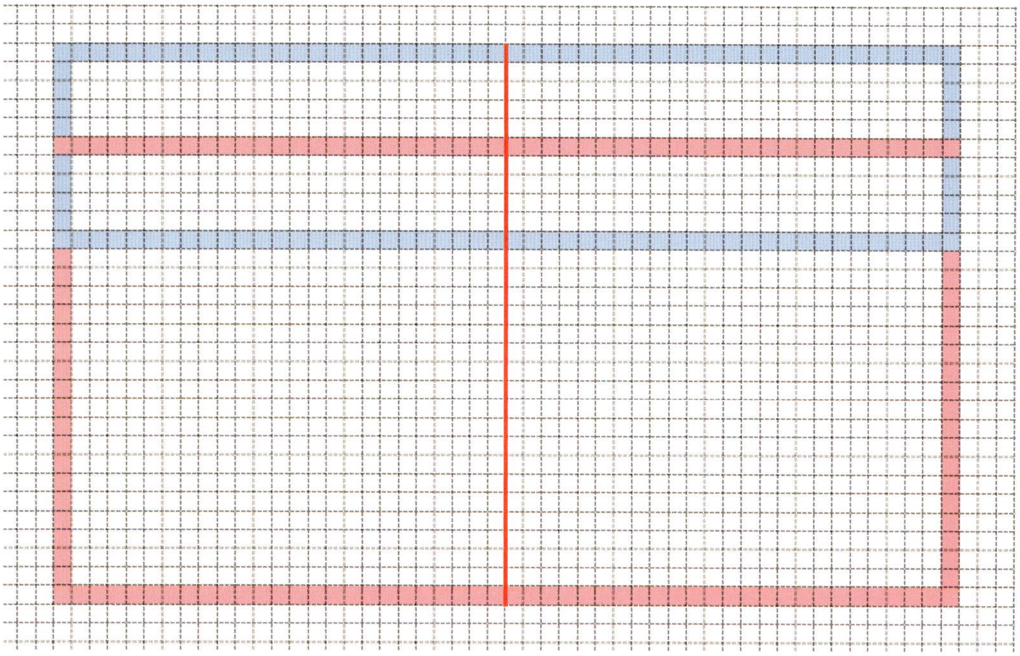

Fig. 9b.

above. This makes a rectangle that is 50 columns wide, and 11 rows high. Mark the center (fig. 9b).

Add a third rectangle for the handle. This rectangle is 10 columns wide and 15 rows high, extending downward on the right, beginning from the horizontal line at the top of the first rectangle (fig. 9c).

### Drafting the Base of the Cup

The next step is to draft a variable curving line to form the base of the cup. Starting at the square to the left of the center at the bottom of the first rectangle, insert a line that extends to the left at 15°, comprising three groups of four filled squares per row. Add each group directly to the left of the previous group, moving upward one row at a time, three rows in total.

Then transition upward at 30°, comprising four groups of two filled squares per row. As before, insert each group directly to the left of the previous group, moving upward one row at a time, four rows in total.

Fig. 9c.

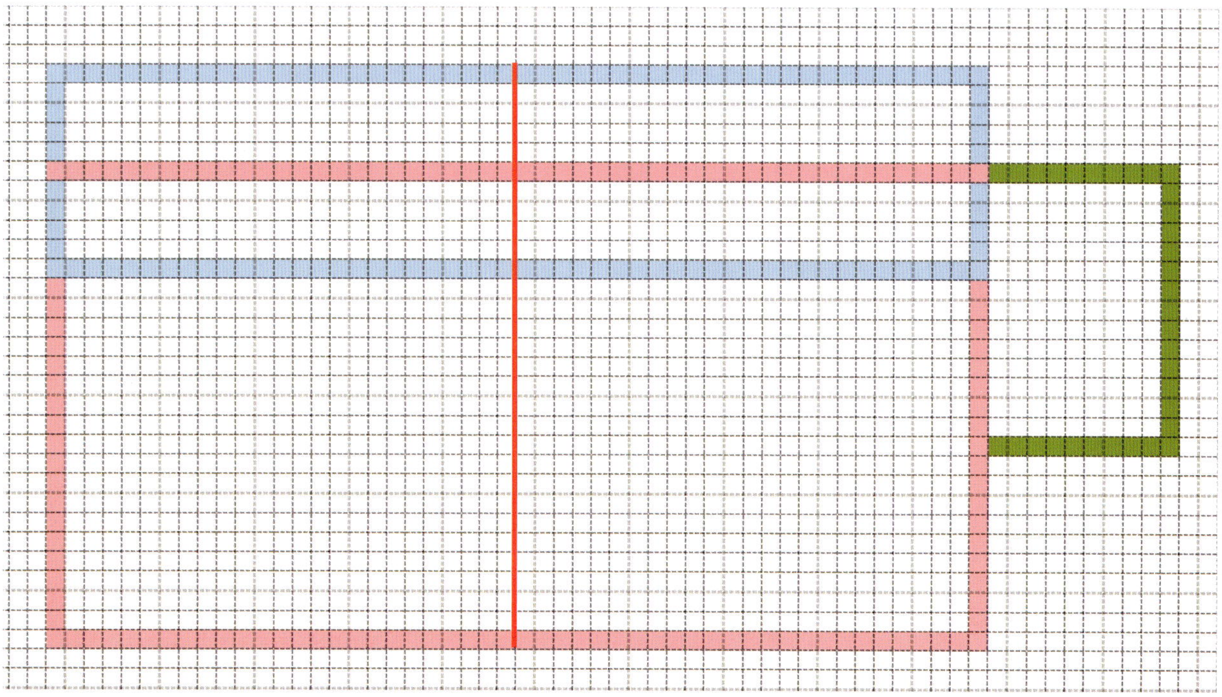

Fig. 9d.

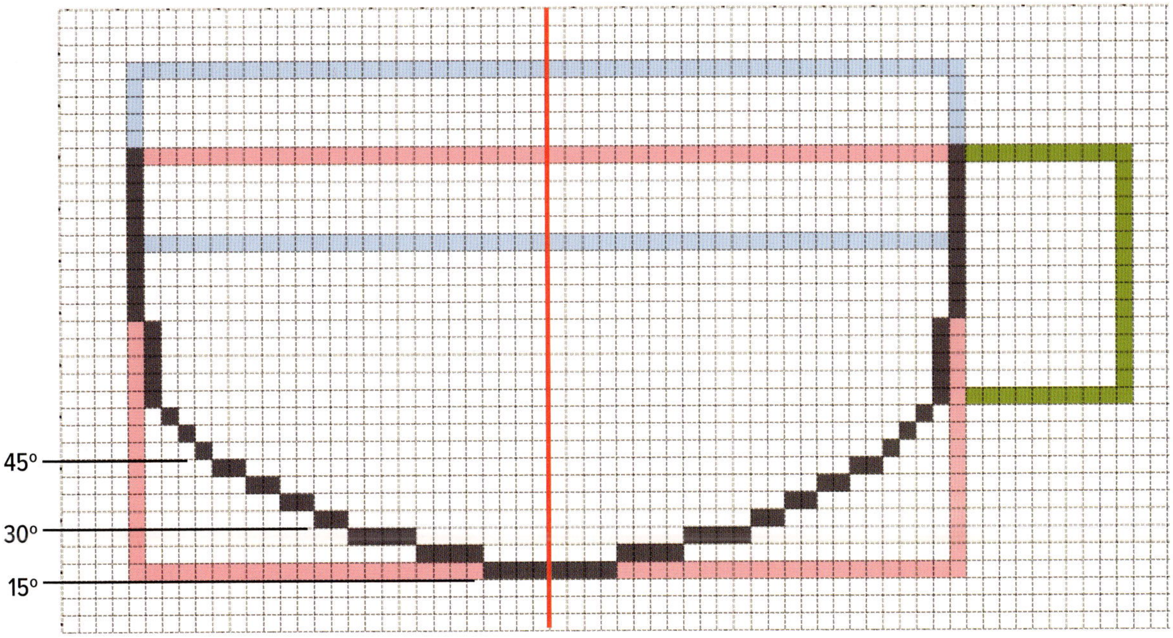


Continue upward with three rows at 45°, inserting one filled square per row, shifting one column to the left with each row, three rows in total.

Following the three rows at 45°, turn upward in the next column to the left, inserting five filled squares one above the other.

Shift one more column to the left and conclude by inserting 10 filled squares one above the other until reaching the top of the first rectangle.

Fashion the right half of the cup's base by turning to the first square to the right of center at the bottom of the rectangle and following the five steps just outlined, reversing the direction of each move in order to replicate the same curve to the right (fig. 9d).

### Drafting the Lip of the Cup

Draft another variable curving line to form the lip of the cup. Starting with the first square to the left of center at the bottom row of the second rectangle, insert a line that extends left at approximately 13°,

Fig. 9e.

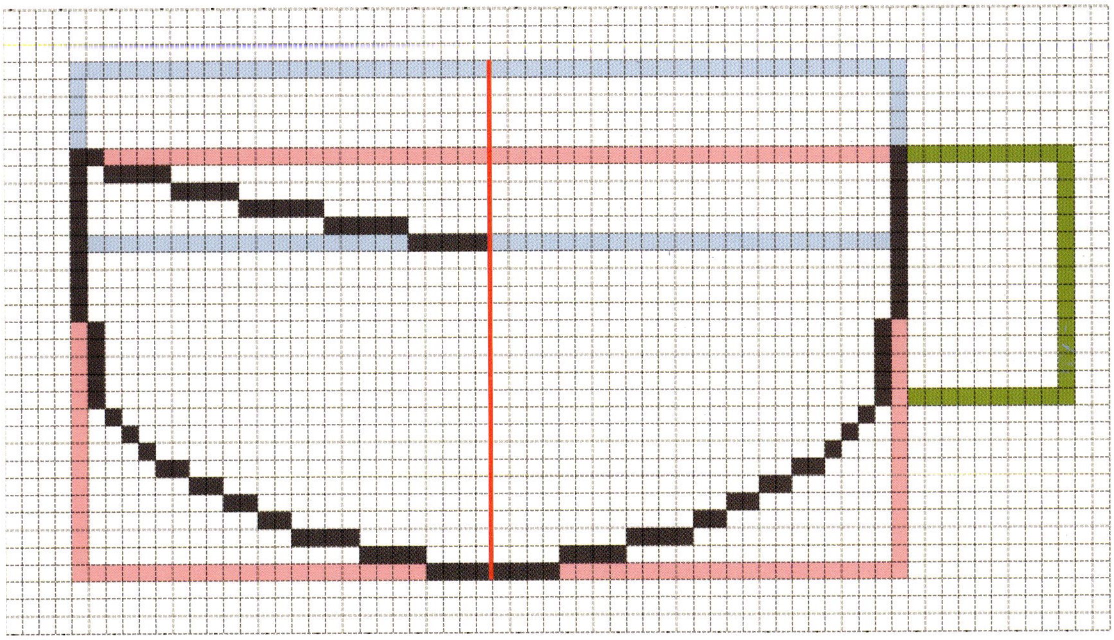

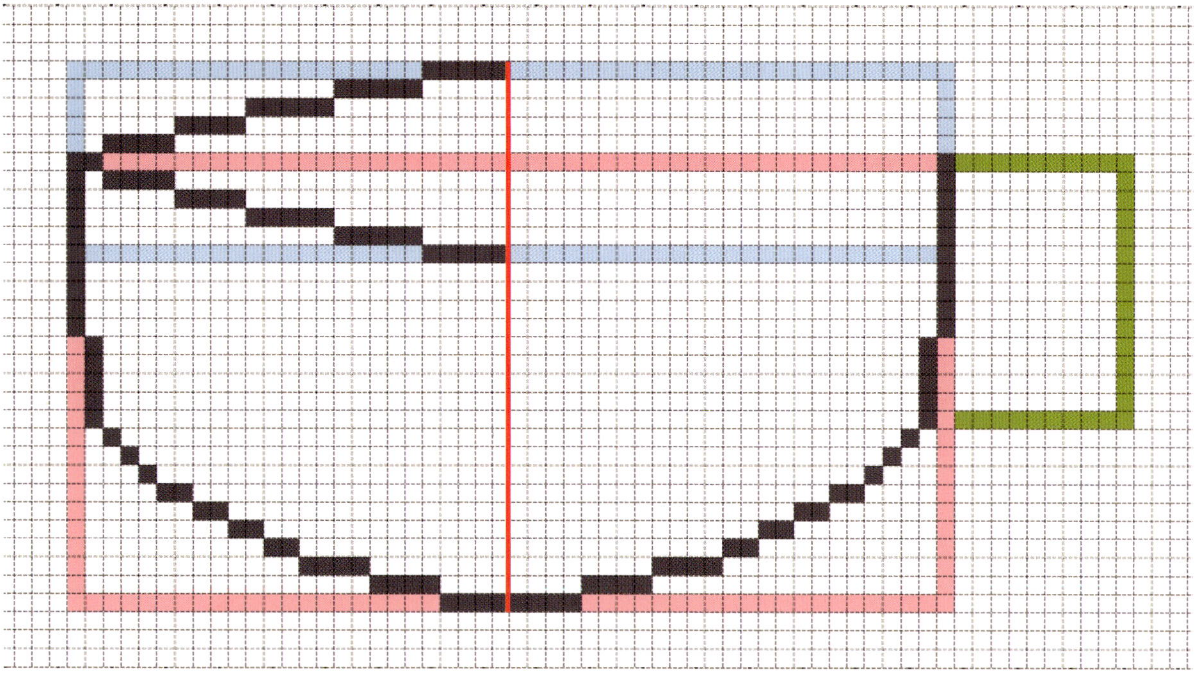

Fig. 9f.

comprising three groups of five filled squares per row. Add each group directly to the left of the previous group, moving upward one row at a time, three rows in total. Continue upward with two rows at 15°, inserting four filled squares per row, adding the second group directly to the left of the first.

Conclude by inserting two filled squares in the next row above, directly to the left of the previous group, thus meeting the top of the first rectangle (fig. 9e).

Complete the left side of the lip as it continues to the back of the cup, working upward to add a second variable curving line directly above the first. Beginning in the next row above, and directly to the right of the two filled squares added in the previous step, insert two groups of four filled squares each, with each group added directly to the right of the previous group, moving upward one row at a time, followed by three groups of five filled squares each. As before, you will add each group directly to the right of the previous group, ending at the top row of the second rectangle (fig. 9f).

For the lip on the right, return to the first square to the right of the midpoint on the bottom row of the second rectangle and retrace the steps outlined under "Drafting the Lip of the Cup," above, reversing the direction of each move in order to complete the cup's opening (fig. 9g).

### Drafting the Handle

Add the outermost edge of the handle by inserting six filled squares at the far right of the rectangle, extending downward consecutively, beginning with the fifth square from the top.

Complete the top of the handle by adding two lines of four filled squares each that converge from right and left at 45°, extending upward to the top of the handle. The 45° line on the right begins one row above the six filled squares that form the handle's outermost edge, offset to the left by one. The 45° line on the left begins on the same row. The two lines will not meet at the top of the handle, and a single filled square must be added to fill the gap.

Fig. 9g.

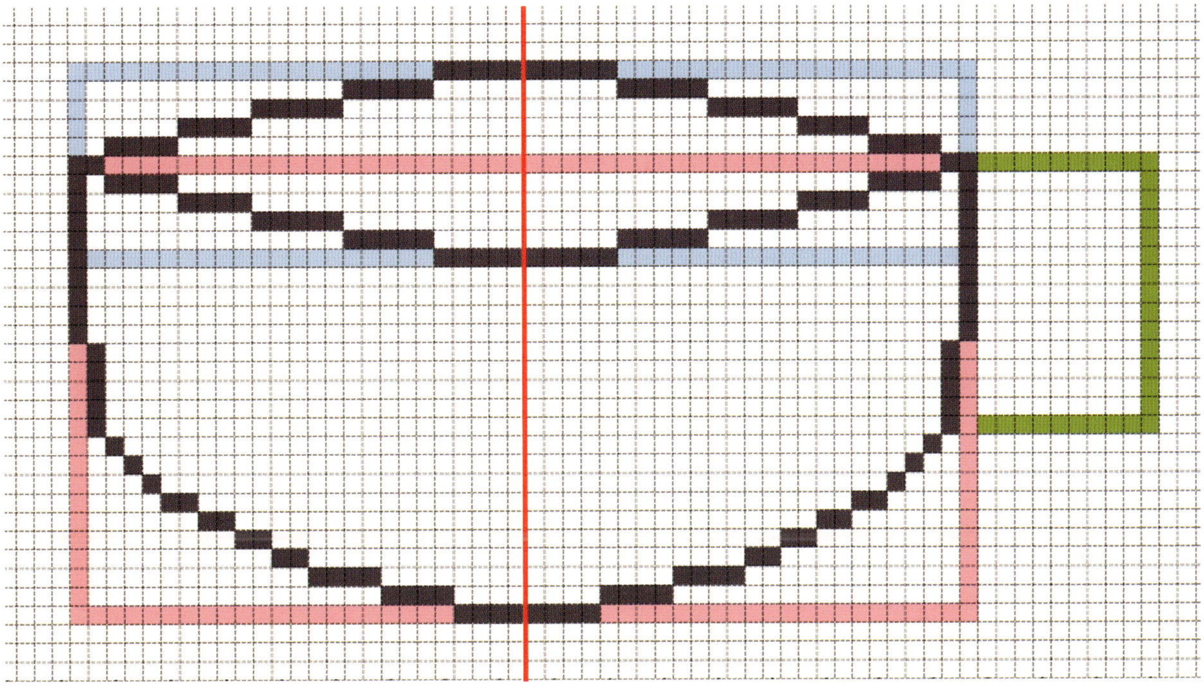

Fig. 9h.

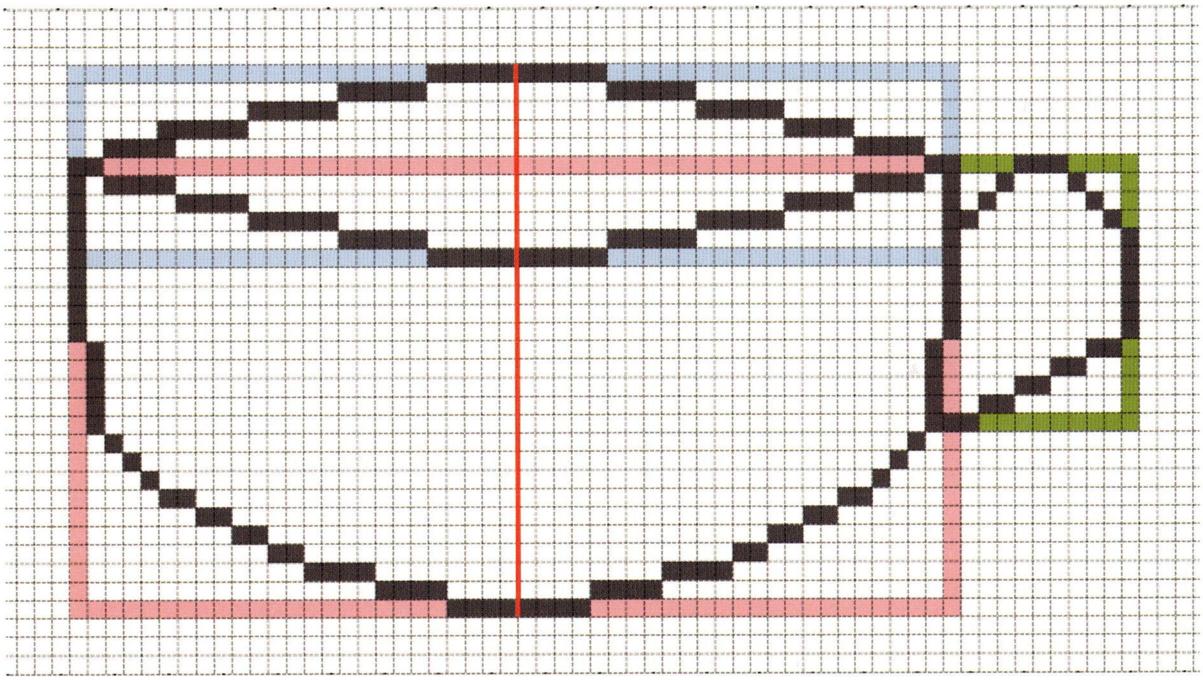

Next, mark the point at the lower left where the bottom of the handle's rectangle joins the cup. Beginning from that point, insert a line that rises at 30° by inserting five groups of two filled squares per row, adding each group directly to the right of thc prcvious group. This 30° line will complete the handle as it reaches the handle's outmost edge (fig. 9h).

You have now drafted the cup's outline. Given that such outlines are often starting points only, other adjustments are needed before the shape reaches its final form. With this cup, the opening above the lip appears diamond shaped rather than rounded. This can be corrected in the draft by moving the center third of the front of the lip downward slightly. This modification will change the curve of the lip, so you also must fine-tune the line on either side to ensure a smooth curve.

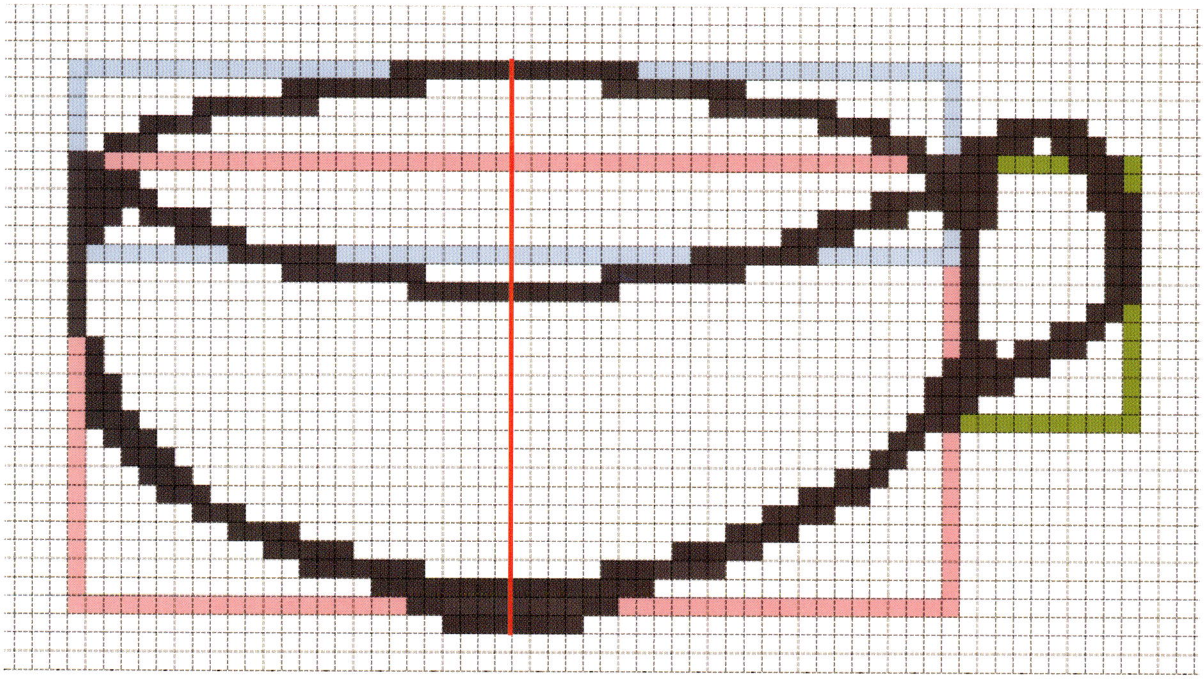

Fig. 9i.

To maintain a symmetrical overall appearance, some modification to the back of the lip may be needed as well.

In addition, the handle seems too low, and the cup lacks a traditional foot at its base. With those corrections made, and a limited amount of shading added at the base, the handle, and the lip, the draft of the cup is now complete (fig. 9i).

As a reminder, the pattern for the cup shown here, which is 60 squares wide, would require 120 warp ends to weave—because only every second warp end is shown on each row of the draft.

## DRAFTING DEMONSTRATION: LETTERS AND WORDS

Squares and rectangles are also effective when drafting smaller forms, such as the letters of the alphabet. To design every letter by using identical or nearly identical squares and rectangles will ensure that they are of similar proportions and will fit together easily.

For this demonstration, the words "coffee break" will be added to the cup already drafted. In addition to pleasant associations for a coffee drinker, these words will also bring a smile to the inlay weaver, because the letters are uncomplicated in form and are sometimes repeated, reducing the amount of work to be done. For variety, this demonstration will use roman rather than italic letters.

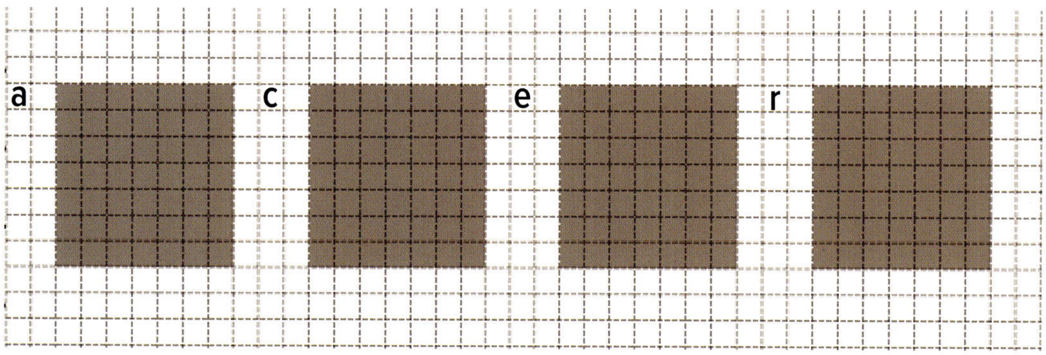


Fig. 10a.

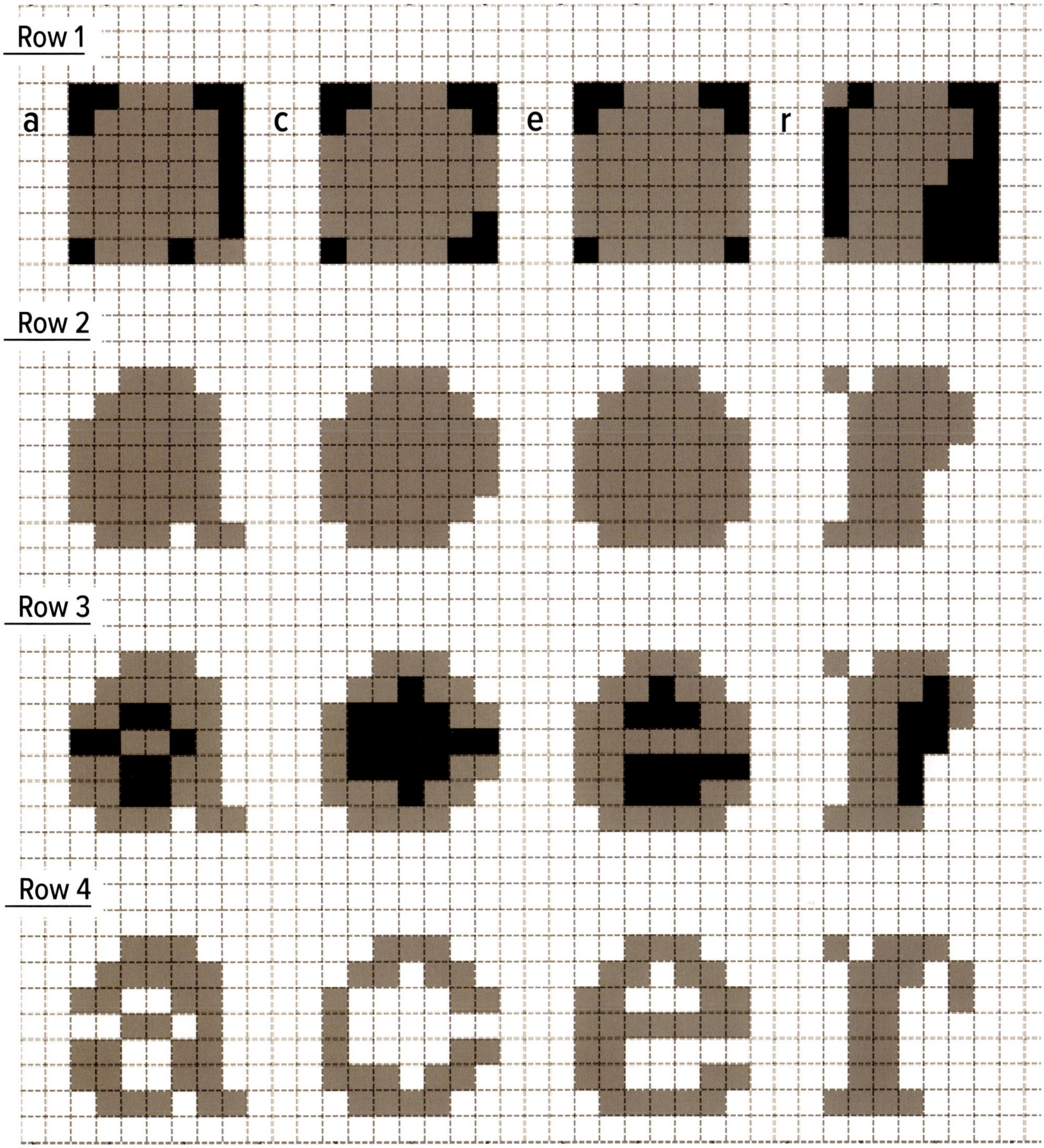


Fig. 10b.

### Drafting *a*, *c*, *e*, and *r*

Following a process somewhat like carving letters in a block of wood, begin by drafting four squares that are each seven rows high and seven columns wide. In this example, the filled squares that make up each shape are shown in gray. In order from left to right, these squares will be the basis for the letters *a*, *c*, *e*, and *r* (fig. 10a).

Starting with row 1 of fig. 10b, remove every black square. The transitional forms that will result are shown in row 2, with the roughly circular forms of the *a*, *c*, and *e* beginning to appear. Then remove the black squares shown in row 3 to open the center of each form. The final form of each letter is shown in row 4.

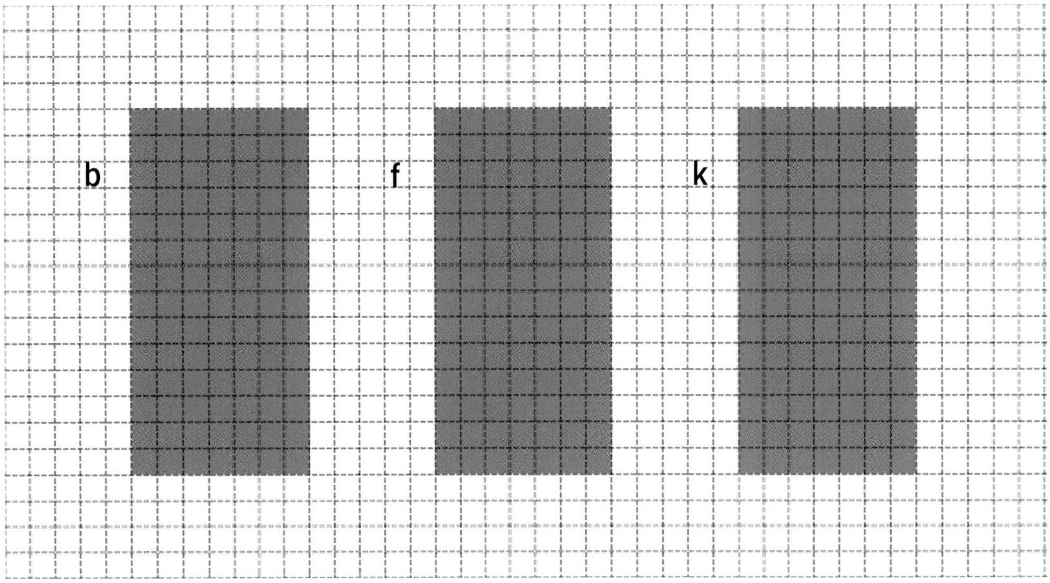


Fig. 10c.

### Drafting *b*, *f*, and *k*

Begin by drafting three rectangles that are 14 rows high and seven columns wide, shown here in gray. These shapes are the basis for the letters *b*, *f*, and *k* (fig. 10c).

Continue by removing the black squares shown in row 1 of fig. 10d. The shapes have temporarily been divided in half to clarify the distinction between the upper and lower parts of each letter. The resulting transitional forms are shown in row 2.

Continue by removing the black squares shown in row 1 of fig. 10e, with the final form of each letter shown in row 2.

### Drafting *o*

Draft five rectangles, each seven rows high and nine columns wide, as the basis for a generously broad *o*. Repeat the process shown with the previous letters, working from left to right in the graphs below (fig. 10f).

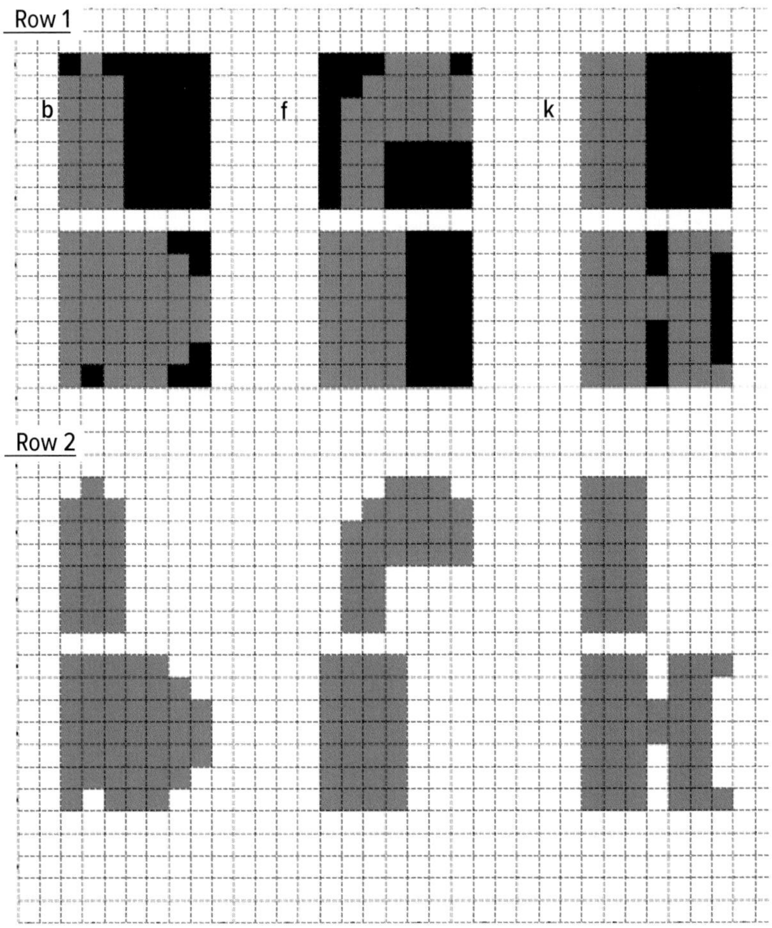


Fig. 10d.

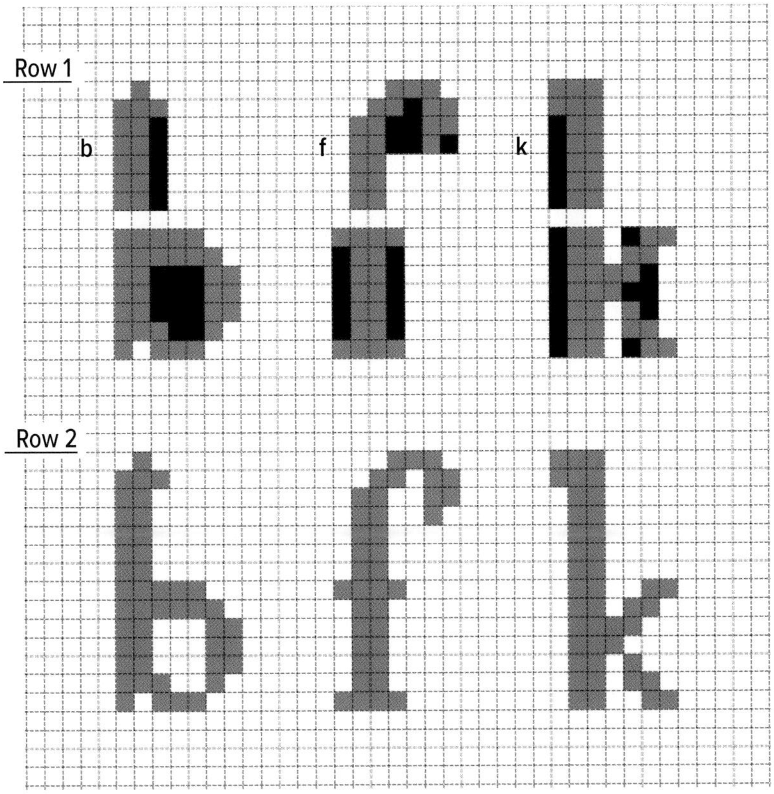


Fig. 10e.

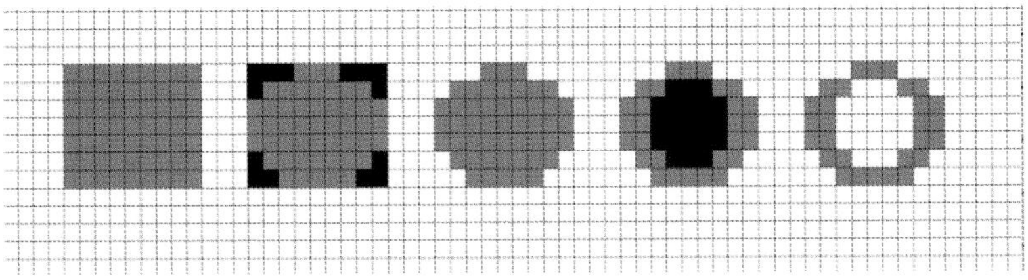

Fig. 10f.

## Spacing Letters and Words

The idiosyncrasies of the letters of the English alphabet make it difficult to formulate hard-and-fast rules for their proper spacing. In general, letters should be spaced closely, but with a clear separation from one letter to the next. The spaces between words should be three to five times that of the spaces between individual letters. The spaces between punctuation marks and letters should be handled in the same way as the spacing of the letters. Regularity and consistency are the goals to be sought when spacing letters and words, avoiding clusters of letters that fit together too tightly, or gaps within or between words.*

These broad guidelines were followed in spacing the letters of the words "coffee break" (fig. 10g), a process made easier by the nearly identical proportions of the letters. In this example, every letter is spaced from the next by one square, and the two

**A rule often found in writing handbooks is that the spaces between letters should match the space between the two legs of the lowercase* n. *Refreshingly, after providing such guidelines, the writers of these handbooks typically encourage readers to avoid* rigid *rules, trusting their own instincts as to what looks best. See A. S. Osley,* Scribes and Sources: Handbook of the Chancery Hand in the Sixteenth Century *(Boston: David R. Godine, 1980).*

Fig. 10g.

words are separated by five squares. The guidelines were set aside briefly to allow the elision of the double *f* of "coffee," a change that saved space without jeopardizing the sense of the word. Serendipitous abbreviations and elisions have long been part of the traditions of penmanship and printing, and such serendipity can be a blessing to the inlay weaver, so long as clarity is preserved and spacing is improved. I feel those criteria were met here.

A satisfactory joining together of an image and words also requires some thought. The goal is a natural, unforced arrangement that causes no discomfort for the viewer, such as the uneasiness felt when words and images are not aligned from right to left or are arranged too close or far from one another. Here, the easiest solution has been followed: The words are centered symmetrically beneath the cup, and the space between the words and the cup is equal to the space between the words themselves.

## DRAFTING DEMONSTRATION: MORE FREEDOM

Legibility and standardization were the goals in the previous demonstration. However, the techniques being described can also be used for irregular shapes that are arranged more freely, such as a design of a flower blowing in the breeze.

### Preparation

As a first step, decide the components of the flower you have in mind. The classic "daisy" often includes an odd number of petals (at least five), a flower disk at the center, a stem, and one or two leaves. For simplicity, one basic petal and one basic leaf can be repeated over and over. However, varying even a few of those shapes will add a great deal of liveliness to the pattern. With that in mind, the flower shown here will have five petals, and those petals will be shaped differently.

### The Petals

Begin by drafting five rectangles and squares according to these criteria:

Two shapes should be large rectangles with 12 rows and 10 columns.

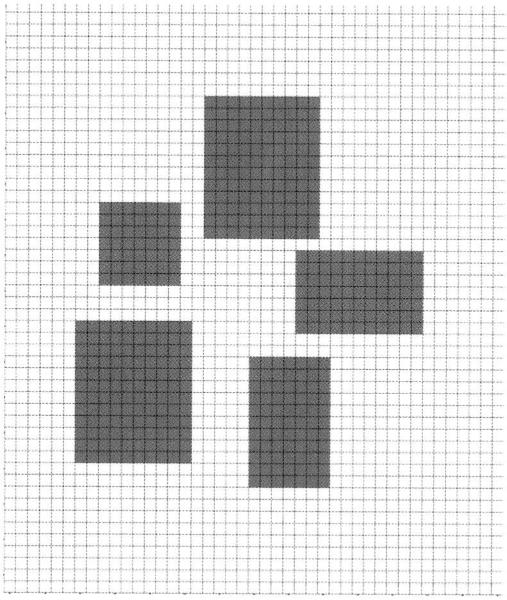

Fig. 11a.

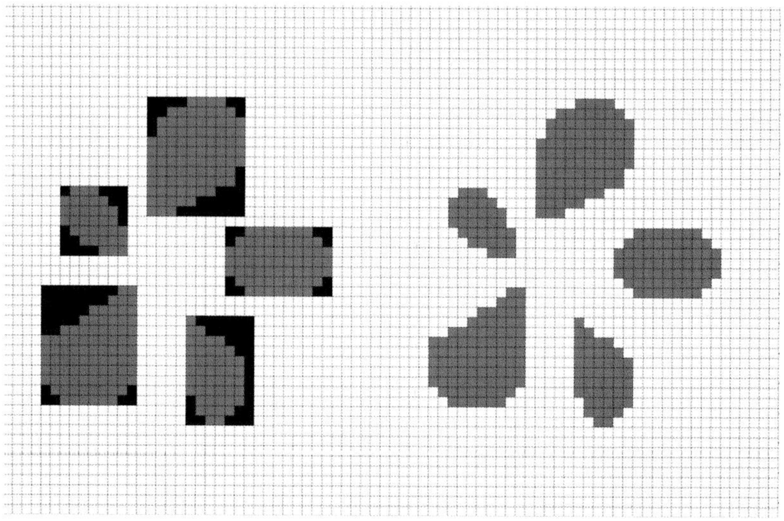

Fig. 11b.

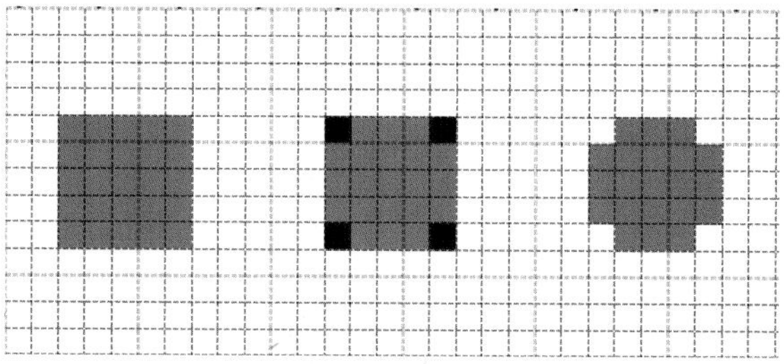

Fig. 11c.

Two shapes should be small rectangles. One of these rectangles should be oriented horizontally, with seven rows and 11 columns. The other rectangle should be oriented vertically, with 11 rows and seven columns.

Fig. 11d.

Fig. 11f.

The fifth shape should be a square with seven rows and seven columns.

Arrange the shapes in a roughly circular pattern of your choosing (fig. 11a).

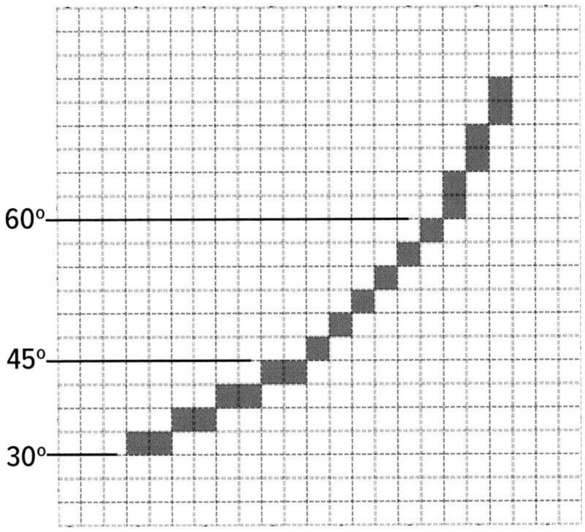


Fig. 11e.

Create the petals by removing three or four corners from each shape. To remove four corners equally will make a stable shape that appears immobile, such as the petal shown at the right (fig. 11b). Removing larger amounts at one or more of the corners will make a sloping shape, as seen in the other four petals shown here. Note that the petals that result from the two smaller rectangles are shaped very differently. After the five petal shapes are complete, they can be repositioned as needed to create a satisfying arrangement.

### The Flower Disk

Draft a small square with five rows and five columns. Then remove the four corners to make a small flower disk (fig. 11c).

Then position the disk in the open space between the petals (fig. 11d).

### The Stem

Fashion the flower's stem by drafting a short variable curving line as follows:

Moving to the right and upward with each insertion, add four rows at 30°, six rows at 45°, and three columns at 60° (fig. 11e).

Then reshape the resulting curve by adding additional filled squares along its entire length to make it more robust, with particular emphasis on the base of the stem. Then place the stem beneath the flower (fig. 11f).

### The Leaves

Fashion two leaves, beginning with horizontal rectangles that each have seven rows and 11 columns (fig. 11g, *left*). Begin by removing large portions from each of the four corners, creating shapes that taper at each end (fig. 11g, *center*). Consider making the two leaves noticeably different in size and slope. Here, one leaf is larger and oriented horizontally, while the other is thinner and slopes upward (fig. 11g, *right*).

Finish the pattern by adding the leaves to the stem (fig. 11h).

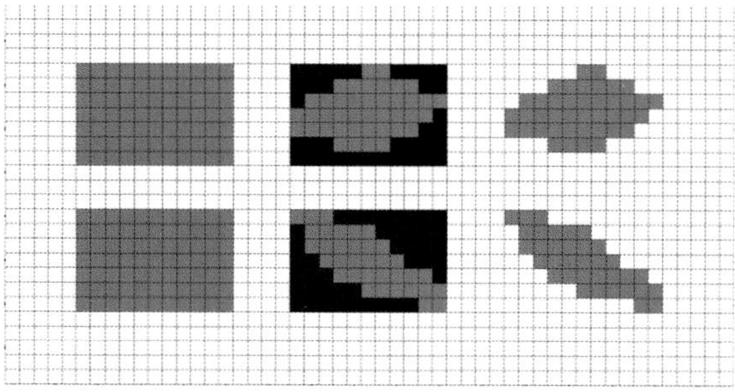

Fig. 11g.

Fig. 11h.

## REVERSING DRAFTS

As described in chapter 1 (see page 19), patterns laid in on the back of the cloth will appear reversed when viewed from the front. For this reason, some drafts must be reversed before weaving.

Spreadsheet programs such as Microsoft Excel provide a way to make drafts electronically, and to reverse those drafts when complete. To do this using Excel, you would do the following:

Narrow the width of the columns contained in a blank workbook to create an electronic chart that resembles graph paper.

Draft a pattern in the graph by filling squares or adding X's or other symbols to indicate where the pattern will be placed in the 1–3 sheds.

Reverse the order of the columns in the workbook, following instructions that can be found online. Your draft will reverse automatically when the columns are reversed (fig. 12).

Fig. 12.

Fig. 13.

Fig. 14.

## NOTATION OF COLOR IN DRAFTS

Specific pattern colors can be notated in a draft through the use of letters, numbers, or symbols. In such cases, a "key" can be given to identify the letters or symbols used to indicate specific colors. As shown in the key in fig. 13, each of the flower's petals is yellow with a red border, the flower disk is brown, and the stem and leaves are green. In other cases, squares are filled with the specific colors to be used, eliminating the need for a key. See also "Laying In Patterns with Color" (page 43).

## USING BACKGROUND WITHOUT PATTERN

In shapes that are filled with laid-in pattern, areas of background without pattern can be used to define different parts of the form. In the draft, these areas without pattern can be shown as dark squares on a light background, or light squares on a dark background. For example, note the eye and the wing of the bird in fig. 14, which indicate the color of the background against the rest of the bird's dark body, and which also contrast the white of the breast and legs. When weaving such patterns, separate pattern strands are needed to lay in the colors on either side of the lines without pattern.

## FREEHAND DRAFTING

Freehand drafting relies on the same straight lines, vertical lines, lines that angle, and curving lines as the step-by-step process described to this point, and those design elements are created in the same way as when working step by step. When you're comfortable drafting these design elements step by step, you will find it easy to adapt those techniques to freehand drafting.

The lamb seen here is a case in point (fig. 15a). The original drawing shows the back and belly as curving pencil lines that are nearly, but not quite, horizontal. They are, in effect, variable curving lines of low degree. The lines that mark the legs and chest are nearly vertical and are best described as angled lines of high degree, although the rear legs transition to approximately 45° as they approach the flanks. The forehead, ears, throat, and nape are drawn as angled and curving lines that vary from 30° to 45° to 60°. While the lines

Fig. 15a, pencil on paper, 11" × 14", 2020

are short and move quickly from one degree to another, they are nevertheless examples of the types of lines described previously under "Design Element: Variable Curving Lines."

The goal when drafting freehand is to identify what is essential about the shape you have imagined, to capture its basic proportions, and to position it as you want it to be seen. With a lamb, we know that the essential qualities are a round belly, legs that are long and gangling, large ears, knees, and hooves, and a head that is a big block. The lamb shown here is positioned simply, directly from the side, but with the legs slightly akimbo, as if it is still unsteady on its feet. The draft is finished when it has captured features like these, and other aspects of a preliminary drawing, such as the shading that provides depth, can be omitted.

Once an image has been drawn satisfactorily, transferring it to a draft is relatively straightforward. If you were to work from the drawing shown in fig. 15a, you would begin by deciding the overall height and width of the finished shape. You would then mark the principal lines that show the proportions of the different parts of the lamb's body, typically drawn as squares and rectangles. For this lamb, the legs could be drawn as narrow, vertical rectangles; the torso as a broad, horizontal rectangle; and the head as a square. As soon as those lines are in place, and the overall proportions of the form appear correct to your eye, you will revise the lines to develop a more complete portrayal. As you work, the pattern will become a web of angling and curving lines. You will find, if you did not know already, that lambs are not made of straight lines, and that virtually every line is in flux at all times. (While this draft began as a sketch on paper, this is not always the case. Many freehand drafts begin at the computer, while clicking squares on a graph with a mouse.)

As your design becomes clear, feel free to allow details from the earlier versions to change or disappear. In the pencil sketch of the lamb, the head is shown in profile, and the ears are raised. Those details appeared in the first woven samples as well. Unfortunately, in those samples the raised ears

Fig. 15b.

made the lamb look fierce and even frightening, which are not characteristics of any lamb I have ever seen. Lowering the lamb's ears, enlarging the eye, and turning the head transformed it from a diabolical monster into something that appears sweet and innocent (fig. 15b).

For readers who doubt their own drawing skills, it should be noted that turning a lamb's head in a sketch or draft is not as difficult as it may sound. If you move the eye and nose in the direction of the turn, shorten the face to add perspective, and draw the base of the distant ear as partly hidden by the head, you will find that the lamb has turned and is looking toward you. While shepherds may say that a newborn lamb is too bleary-eyed for this behavior, I find the immediacy of the gesture to be poignant, and it has become the single most important feature of the design. Having discovered this quality, I repeated it again and again, and in a series of drawings and drafts that followed, the lamb often turns to look outward (fig. 15c–d). For me, the lesson learned is that once you find something that engages your imagination, such as the expressiveness of a lamb turning toward you, it can be repeated as often as you want without monotony—because the laws of human nature say that it will be fresh for others as long as it remains fresh for you.

Fig. 15c, pencil on paper, 11" × 14", 2020

Fig. 15d.

OPPOSITE:

*Daniel Janes*, 18" × 28", linen, 2023, detail

together

beginnings

— *Chapter 3* —

# PROJECTS

## GENERAL INSTRUCTIONS FOR THE PROJECTS

### PREPARING THE LOOM

For each project, use the following draft to dress and treadle your loom.

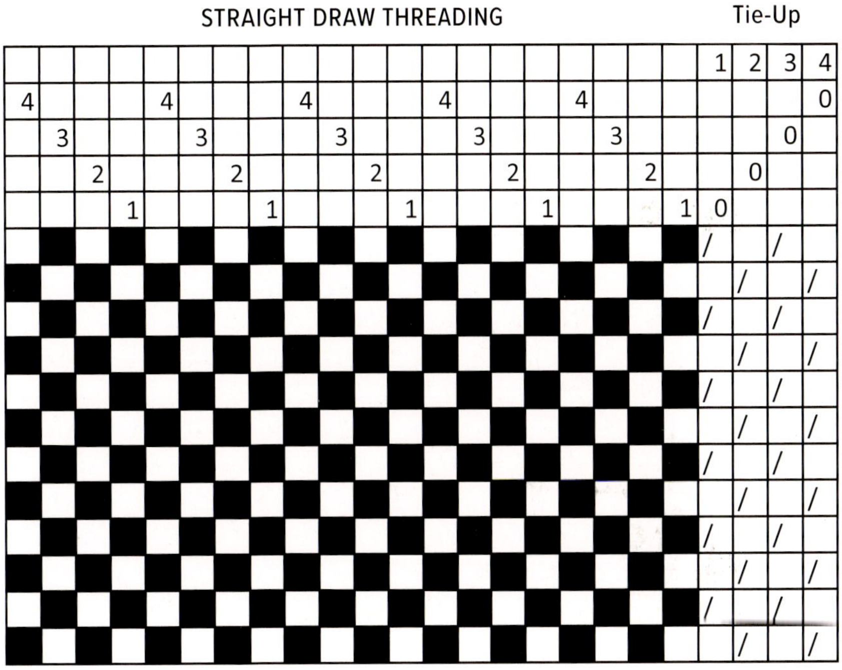


### LAYING IN AN IMAGE

Most of the projects in this chapter combine images with words or phrases (a few of the projects consist of images alone). The process for laying in an image is similar to that of a letter or word, and the relevant sections from chapter 1 can be reviewed as a general introduction. However, there are differences when laying in an image, which are usually larger in size and often require you to manage multiple strands and colors simultaneously.

As an example, turn to the draft for the project titled Beginning. Disregard the laid-in text for now and consider the steps described here only in relation to the duckling emerging from its egg.

## THE FIRST 1–3 SHED

Open the 1–3 shed and mark the center of the warp. For warps with widths that are odd numbers—such as the warp for Beginning—there will be a single raised warp end at the center. For warps of even-numbered widths, the center will fall between two raised warp ends. Then identify the center of the pattern indicated in the draft, and plot the starting points for the pattern by counting the squares horizontally to the right or left that separate each starting point from the center.

When looking at the pattern for the duckling and its egg, you will see that the pattern is 155 squares wide, with the center found at the 78th square. The two starting points—the bottom of each half of the egg—are found 55 squares to the left of the center (counted as 55 raised warp ends), and 49 squares (49 raised warp ends) to the right of the center.

Starting with the left half of the egg, begin by locating the 55th raised warp end to the left of the center of the warp. (Exclude from this count the raised warp end at the center of the pattern.) Pass a strand of brown linen under eight raised warp ends in total, including the warp end you have just identified, as well as the seven warp ends to its left. Leave a short tail at the left and bring the remainder of the strand upward to the right, to carry over to the next shed. (As has been the practice throughout this book, you will continue to pass the pattern strands from left to right in the 1–3 sheds, and right to left in the 2–4 sheds.)

Continuing with the right half of the egg, locate the 49th raised warp end to the right of the center. (Again, exclude from this count the raised warp end at the center of the pattern.) Pass a strand of brown linen under the warp end you have just identified, as well as the 11 raised warp ends to its right (12 warp ends total). Leave a tail at the left and bring the remainder of the strand upward to the right, to carry over to the next shed.

Double-check for accuracy and secure each strand to the warp by looping or knotting its tail. Throw a pick of background yarn in the same shed, beat the pattern strands and the background together, close the shed, and open the 2–4 shed.

## THE 2–4 SHED

Still working with the right half of the egg, refer to the draft and note that the pattern will expand outward in both directions in the next 1–3 shed, creating a broad, wedge-like shape similar to the shape described in fig. 5 of "A Guide to Inlay in the 2–4 Sheds" (chapter 1). Begin that outward expansion by passing the pattern strand under 13 raised warp ends, including the warp ends immediately to the right and left of the pattern in the 1–3 shed just completed, as well as the 11 warp ends in between. Note that the outward expansion of this pattern shape will cause a pattern float that would span four raised warp ends prior to the next 1–3 shed. Therefore, this strand should be secured with a loop or knot and trimmed. (The brown outline of the right half of the egg will be continued by a new pattern strand in the next 1–3 shed.)

Looking at the left half of the egg, you will see that, as with the right, the pattern will expand outward in a wedge-like shape in the next 1–3 shed. Begin that outward expansion by passing the pattern strand under nine raised warp ends, including the warp ends immediately to the right and left of the pattern in the 1–3 shed just completed, as well as the seven warp ends in between.

Note that the pattern float that will occur prior to the next 1–3 shed is relatively short and can be ignored.

Bring the remainder of the strand upward to be carried over, throw a pick of the background yarn, beat, and open the second 1–3 shed.

## THE SECOND 1–3 SHED

Beginning with the left half of the egg, three pattern strands, labeled (a), (b), and (c) below, will be used as follows:

Strand (a): Pass the existing brown strand under four raised warp ends, including the leftmost warp end used for the pattern in the previous 1–3 shed, as well as the three warp ends to its left. Bring the strand upward to be carried over.

Strand (b): Pass a new strand of white linen under six raised warp ends in total, beginning with the warp end immediately to the right of strand (a). Leave a tail at the left and bring the strand upward to be carried over.

Strand (c): Pass a new strand of brown linen under seven raised warp ends in total, beginning with the warp end immediately to the right of strand (b). Leave a tail at the left and bring the strand upward to be carried over.

For the right half of the egg, three pattern strands, labeled (d), (e), and (f) below, will be used as follows:

Strand (d): Pass a new strand of brown linen under five raised warp ends, including the leftmost warp end used for the pattern in the previous 1–3 shed, as well as the four warp ends to its left. Leave a tail at the left and bring the strand upward to be carried over.

Strand (e): Pass a new strand of white linen under 10 warp ends in total, beginning with the raised warp end immediately to the right of strand (d). Leave a tail at the left and bring the strand upward to be carried over.

Strand (f): Pass a new strand of brown linen under four raised warp ends in total, beginning with the warp end immediately to the right of strand (e). Leave a tail at the left and bring the strand upward to be carried over.

Double-check for accuracy, then secure each of the five new strands to the warp by looping or knotting the tails. Throw a pick of background yarn, beat, and open the 2–4 shed.

## THE 2–4 SHED

Beginning with the right half of the egg, take the six pattern strands of the previous shed in reverse order as follows:

Strand (f): Note that strand (f) will continue moving to the right in the next 1–3 shed. Refer to fig. 3b in chapter 1's "A Guide to Inlay." Then pass the pattern strand under the raised warp end immediately to the right of the right-hand warp end used for pattern in the 1–3 shed just completed, as well as the next three warp ends to the left (four warp ends total).

Strand (e): Note that the center of the pattern carried by strand (e) will expand outward in both directions in a wedge-like shape in the next 1–3 shed. Refer to fig. 5 in chapter 1's "A Guide to Inlay." Then pass the strand under 11 raised warp ends, including the warp ends immediately to the right and left of the pattern in the 1–3 shed just completed, as well as the nine warp ends in between.

Strand (d): Note that strand (d) will continue moving to the left in the next 1–3 shed. Refer to fig. 3a in chapter 1's "A Guide to Inlay." Then pass the strand under the raised warp end immediately to the left of the right-hand warp end used for pattern in the 1–3 shed just completed, as well as the next four warp ends to the left (five warp ends total).

Continue with the left half of the egg as follows:

Strand (c): Note that strand (c) will continue moving to the right in the next 1–3 shed. Refer to fig. 3b in chapter 1's "A Guide to Inlay." Then pass the pattern strand under the raised warp end immediately to the right of the right-hand warp end used for pattern in the 1–3 shed just completed, as well as the next six warp ends to the left (seven warp ends total).

Strand (b): Note that the center of the pattern carried by strand (b) will expand outward in both directions in a wedge-like shape in the next 1–3 shed. Refer to fig. 5 in chapter 1's "A Guide to Inlay." Then pass the pattern strand under seven raised warp ends, including the warp ends immediately to the right and left of the pattern in the 1–3 shed just completed, as well as the five warp ends in between.

Strand (a): Note that strand (a) will continue moving to the left in the next 1–3 shed. Refer to fig. 3a in chapter 1's "A Guide to Inlay." Then pass the strand under the raised warp end immediately to the left of the right-hand warp end used for pattern in the 1–3 shed just completed, as well as the next three warp ends to the left (four warp ends total).

Bring each of the six pattern strands upward to be carried over. Throw a pick of background yarn, beat, and open the third 1–3 shed.

From this point forward, continue laying in the pattern in the same way as just described. The following details should be noted as you progress through the pattern:

Given that every horizontal row of the draft represents an open 1–3 shed, you will begin laying in the duckling's left foot in the seventh 1–3 shed, and the duckling's body in the 11th 1–3 shed. You could determine the placement of these pattern shapes by counting raised warp ends to the right and left of the center, as in other patterns described previously. However, it can be difficult to locate the precise center of a densely worked pattern once the laying in has begun. A more reliable method is to count raised warp ends from another part of the pattern that has been inserted nearby in the same shed. In the seventh 1–3 shed, for example, you would first lay in the brown pattern strand outlining the half of the egg that is positioned nearest to the foot. Then you would count raised warp ends beginning from the first raised warp end to the right of the brown pattern just inserted to identify the foot's precise placement. In looking at the draft, you will find that the pattern strand for the duckling's foot is inserted under the 25th through the 31st raised warp ends (seven warp ends total) to the right of the egg.

At least three pattern strands will be needed at any given time for each pattern shape, including the duckling's body and the two halves of the egg. Typically, two strands of brown linen will be needed to outline each shape, plus a single white or yellow strand to fill the shape. In some cases, the number of strands will increase. For example, three brown strands and two yellow strands are needed to lay in the area around the duckling's eye, four brown strands and two white strands are needed to lay in some of the jagged portions of the egg on the left, and as many as eight strands are needed to lay in the duckling's body, wing, and feet simultaneously (five brown strands, one orange strand, and two yellow strands).

The pattern includes broad expanses that are filled with laid-in pattern, including the yellow of the duckling and the white of the two halves of the egg. Longer pattern strands are needed for these sections, and firm beating is required. (For more on this subject, see "Working with Pattern Strands" on page 39 and "Beating Inlaid Patterns" on page 39.) These strands will diminish quickly in length and will be replaced frequently due to the broad spans being covered.

Some experimentation may be necessary to determine the best weight for the yarn to be used for the pattern. As noted in "The Weight of the Pattern Weft" (page 38), it can be effective when laying in a pattern using 40/2 linen to insert a doubled strand of 40/2 linen in each 1–3 shed, and a single strand in each 2–4 shed. As with other aspects of woven inlay, to sample first is a reliable way to achieve a good final result.

## WEAVING WITH LINEN

As a reminder, a range of fibers and weights are suitable for woven inlay, depending on the final effect you are aiming for. I prefer linen when weaving inlay, for several reasons. First, like most weavers, I find the lovely sheen of linen when ironed to be irresistible. Second, cloth woven from linen is generally tough and durable, providing an element of permanence that is reassuring, given the many hours we spend laying in the patterns. Finally, linen provides a crisp finish that is very different in appearance from cloth woven in wool or other "fuzzy" yarns (even silk can appear fuzzy when compared to tightly spun linen). Due to this crispness, patterns laid in using linen tend to be clear and well defined, particularly when woven using finer weights. For these reasons, 40/2 linen is the fiber used throughout this book.

Yarn substitutions are possible in the projects that follow. However, if you choose to weave with a fiber other than linen, take care to account for the differences that may result, including the number of warp ends per inch, the size of the laid-in pattern, the overall width of the item, and whether the fiber you have chosen can be beaten firmly into place. For example, it would be possible to weave any of the following projects using 20/2 cotton (sett at 20 e.p.i.) rather than 40/2 linen (sett at 32 e.p.i.). However, the laid-in pattern will grow longer and wider when woven in 20/2 cotton. And given the increased thickness of 20/2 cotton when compared with 40/2 linen, the total number of warp ends must be decreased, to keep the overall width of the item within the parameters of the project. As a result of these factors, the laid-in pattern will cover a larger area of the final item when woven, when compared to the original version using 40/2 linen. Finally, different fibers behave differently when washed and dried, which might affect the appearance of the laid-in pattern when completed. For all these reasons, when making yarn substitutions it is a good idea to weave a sample of the pattern in advance.

To return to linen, a few suggestions may be helpful to those who have not yet explored this versatile, beautiful, but sometimes difficult fiber. Linen's reputation for difficulty originates from the fact that it is often brittle and nonelastic. This brittleness can lead to a higher-than-expected number of broken warp ends while weaving. In addition, plied linen (such as the 40/2 linen used here) tends to twist into knots. These difficulties are magnified by linen's relative fineness—meaning that when weaving with linen, you're working with many more warp ends and weft picks that when weaving with heavier yarns. This increases the likelihood that problems—and frustration—will arise.

Steps to address broken warps ends are discussed under "Broken Warp Ends" (page 40). These steps include often advancing the warp to reduce tension and wear and tear at the selvages, limiting draw-in by leaving short loops of weft at the selvages with every pick, and lightly dampening the warp with water.

## WHILE WINDING AND BEAMING A WARP

Linen's tendency to twist into knots is most prevalent at times when there is no tension on the fiber, such as when winding or beaming a warp. At those times, it is helpful to work with "soft hands," handling the linen calmly and without hurry and avoiding hard tugs that can pull a simple twist into a tight, inflexible knot. When winding or beaming a warp, allow the linen to pass through your hands easily, with no more pressure than needed to keep the linen in place. It can be helpful to shake the linen gently as it passes through your hands, with the gentle shaking eliminating many minor tangles before they have a chance to create more significant problems.

When beaming a warp, work with small batches of warp at a time, rather than gathering the entire warp together into a large clump. Stand or sit far back from the loom, allowing 4 or 5 feet of warp to stretch in front of you. Spread the warp open from left to right. As you spread the warp, many individual tangles will become apparent to your eye. Untangle the twists closest to you and then gently pull the warp snug, shaking as you pull. Continue working across the warp in this manner, taking time to address every tangle that appears. Check for additional tangles at the cross by pulling a section of warp gently taut with one hand while sliding the lease sticks forward and backward with the other hand. Any remaining twists will appear as the warp slides through the lease sticks. Always beam the warp slowly and steadily, watching for any significant tangles that catch in the lease sticks. In the case of a serious tangle, pause to remove the twist before continuing.

Finally, when winding a warp, use a one-by-one rather than a two-by-two cross. This will limit the ability of individual warp ends to twist with their neighbors.

## WHILE WEAVING

As a fiber, linen is somewhat stiff and prone to sliding out of place when not held under tension. While weaving, this tendency can allow linen to slip off the shaft of the bobbin as the shuttle passes through the shed, creating tangles inside the shuttle that catch and stop the shuttle's forward momentum. This problem can be addressed by lifting the shuttle upward—above your head—before throwing it through each shed, an action that causes a length of weft yarn that is longer than the width of the warp to wind from the bobbin. As a result, the shuttle will exit from the opposite shed, even if a snag occurs at the bobbin. Some practice will be needed to develop consistency in terms of the length of weft prior to throwing the shuttle with every shed.

In addition, develop the habit of using your finger to stop the bobbin from spinning as soon as the shuttle exits the shed, thus preventing excess weft yarn from unwinding from a bobbin that continues to spin. It is also helpful to wind the yarn onto the bobbins in an exaggerated "football" shape, putting most of the yarn at the center of the bobbin, and considerably less yarn at either end of the shaft. To avoid overloading the bobbins will also reduce the likelihood of linen yarn slipping off the shaft of the bobbin as the shuttle passes through the shed.

Bockens 35/2 linen lace yarn provides a range of colors that are well suited to laying in patterns when working with 40/2 or other finer weights of linen. Bockens linen lace yarn is available from Vävstuga Weaving School, www.vavstuga.com.

Beginning

# BEGINNING

## *Project:* DISH TOWEL

### PREPARATION

**Weave structure:** plain weave

**Warp and weft:** 40/2 linen in natural, 6,000 yards per pound

**Sett:** 32 ends per inch

**Number of warp ends:** 641

**Width in the reed:** 20"

**Warp length:** Wind a 3-yard warp in natural linen for one dish towel plus extra for sampling and loom waste. When weaving multiple dish towels, add an extra yard to the warp (requiring an additional 1,280 yards for warp and weft combined) for each additional towel as follows:

- 3-yard warp, one towel: 3,840 yards in total for warp and weft, 10½ oz. by weight (excluding the linen used for the pattern)
- 4-yard warp, two towels: 5,120 yards (13½ oz. by weight)
- 5-yard warp, three towels: 6,400 yards (1 lb., 1 oz. by weight)

**Loom preparation:** Dress and treadle for plain weave

**Pattern colors/yardage for one dish towel using 40/2 linen (allowing for doubled strands and waste):** green (50 yards), medium brown (40 yards), white (70 yards), yellow (60 yards), orange (8 yards)

### WEAVING THE PROJECT AND LAYING IN THE PATTERN

Review the General Instructions for the Projects.

As noted in the General Instructions, the pattern is 155 columns wide (equaling 155 raised warp ends), with the center of the pattern at the 78th column. Use Natural linen for the background weft. Begin each dish towel by weaving a header, 3" in length. Continue by laying in the pattern, centered in the warp. After laying in, the pattern itself will be approximately 9" in length. Finish by weaving to a total length of 30".

Weave additional dish towels if planned. Then remove from the loom and finish by stitching raw ends, washing in cold water, air drying, ironing (hot iron, steam setting), and hemming.

Approximate finished dimensions of one dish towel after hemming:

**Width:** 18½"

**Length:** 25½"

together

# TOGETHER

*Project:*
## DISH TOWEL

### PREPARATION

**Weave structure:** plain weave

**Warp and weft:** 40/2 linen in natural, 6,000 yards per pound

**Sett:** 32 ends per inch

**Number of warp ends:** 640

**Width in the reed:** 20"

**Warp length:** Wind a 3-yard warp in natural linen for one dish towel plus extra for sampling and loom waste. When weaving multiple dish towels, add an extra yard to the warp (requiring an additional 1,280 yards for warp and weft combined) for each additional towel as follows:

- 3-yard warp, one towel: 3,840 yards in total for warp and weft, 10½ oz. by weight (excluding the linen used for the pattern)
- 4-yard warp, two towels: 5,120 yards (13½ oz. by weight)
- 5-yard warp, three towels: 6,400 yards (1 lb., 1 oz. by weight)

**Loom preparation:** Dress and treadle for plain weave

**Pattern colors/yardage for one dish towel using 40/2 linen (allowing for doubled strands and waste):** pink (105 yards), bright red (30 yards), medium brown (80 yards), white (100 yards)

### WEAVING THE PROJECT AND LAYING IN THE PATTERN

**Review the General Instructions for the Projects.**

The pattern is 108 columns wide (equaling 108 raised warp ends), with the center of the pattern found at the vertical line between the 54th and 55th columns. Use Natural linen for the background weft. Begin each dish towel by weaving a header, 3" in length. Continue by laying in the pattern, centered in the warp. After laying in, the pattern itself will be approximately 9" in length. Finish by weaving to a total length of 30".

Weave additional dish towels if planned. Then remove from the loom and finish by stitching raw ends, washing in cold water, air drying, ironing (hot iron, steam setting), and hemming.

Approximate finished dimensions of one dish towel after hemming:

**Width:** 18½"

**Length:** 25½"

### PROJECT NOTES

This project's word follows the arching shape of the banner, with no two letters placed on the same horizontal row of the draft. Nevertheless, the basic principles for planning and laying in these letters will remain the same as those found in chapter 1.

Unlike the other projects, where words or phrases appear against a plain-weave background only, this word is placed on a background that is laid in with white. A varying number of white and medium-brown pattern strands will be needed to lay in the banner and the word, depending on the complexity of the letters at any given point in the pattern. As many as 12 medium-brown strands and 11 white strands will be in use at the same time, requiring some diligence to prevent tangled strands.

The corners at the bottom of the banner drop downward and are laid in simultaneously with the lower portion of the heart. To bring your attention to the corners at the proper time, highlight their starting points in the draft in advance.

# BIRD LOVER'S TEATIME

*Project:*
**NAPKINS**

## PREPARATION

**Weave structure:** plain weave

**Warp:** 40/2 linen in natural, 6,000 yards per pound

**Weft:** 40/2 linen in white, 6,000 yards per pound

**Sett:** 32 ends per inch

**Number of warp ends:** 576

**Width in the reed:** 18"

**Warp length:** Wind a 4-yard warp in natural linen for four napkins plus extra for sampling and loom waste. In total, 4,608 yards of linen (12½ oz. by weight) will be required for warp and weft combined (excluding the linen used for the pattern).

**For eight napkins, wind a 6-yard warp:** 6,912 yards (1 lb., 3 oz. by weight)

**Loom preparation:** Dress and treadle for plain weave

**Pattern colors/yardage for four napkins using 40/2 linen (allowing for doubled strands and waste):** black (220 yards), pink (60 yards), dark brown (40 yards), white (100 yards)

## WEAVING THE PROJECT AND LAYING IN THE PATTERN

Review the General Instructions for the Projects.

The pattern is 74 columns wide (equaling 74 raised warp ends), with the center of the pattern found at the vertical line between the 37th and 38th columns. Use white linen for the background weft. Begin each napkin by weaving a header, 2" in length. Continue by laying in the pattern, centered in the warp. After laying in, the pattern itself will be approximately 4½" in length. Finish by weaving to a total length of 20".

Weave additional napkins if planned. Then remove from the loom and finish by stitching raw ends, washing in cold water, air drying, ironing (hot iron, steam setting), and hemming.

Approximate finished dimensions of one napkin after hemming:

**Width:** 17½"

**Length:** 16½"

## PROJECT NOTES

The bird's eye and wing are areas where no pattern is inserted, with the woven background alone providing a light highlight against the black body and head. See "Using Background Without Pattern" in chapter 2.

"drink
your
tea!"

# BIRD LOVER'S TEATIME

## *Project:* TEA COZY*

### PREPARATION

**Weave structure:** plain weave

**Warp:** 40/2 linen in natural, 6,000 yards per pound

**Weft:** 40/2 linen in white, 6,000 yards per pound

**Sett:** 32 ends per inch

**Number of warp ends:** 576

**Width in the reed:** 18"

**Warp length:** Wind a 3-yard warp in natural linen for one tea cozy front panel and one back panel, plus extra for sampling and loom waste. When weaving multiple tea cozies, add an extra yard to the warp (requiring an additional 1,152 yards of linen for the warp and weft combined) for each additional cozy as follows:

- 3-yard warp, one cozy: 3,456 yards in total for warp and weft, 9½ oz. by weight (excluding the linen used for the pattern)
- 4-yard warp, two cozies: 4,608 yards (12½ oz. by weight)
- 5-yard warp, three cozies: 5,760 yards of linen (16 oz. by weight)

**Loom preparation:** Dress and treadle for plain weave

**Colors/yardage for the one front and one back panel using 40/2 linen (allowing for doubled pattern strands and waste):** pink (25 yards for front panel, 500 yards for back panel), black (115 yards for front panel only) dark brown (80 yards for front panel, 500 yards for back panel), white (25 yards for front panel, 400 yards for back panel)

OPPOSITE:

Teapot by Tiffany Hilton;
cup by Hashi Pottery

**The phrase "Drink your tea!" is a mnemonic used by birdwatchers to identify the call of the Eastern Towhee, a black songbird with vivid rust-and-white markings.*

### WEAVING THE PROJECT AND LAYING IN THE PATTERN

Review the General Instructions for the Projects.

For the front panel: The pattern is 176 columns wide (equaling 176 raised warp ends), with the center of the pattern found at the vertical line between the 88th and 89th columns. Use white linen for the background weft. Begin by weaving a header, 3" in length. Continue by laying in the pattern, centered in the warp. After laying in, the pattern itself will be approximately 8" in length. Finish by weaving to a total length of 16".

For the back panel: Repeat the following color order in the weft to a length of approximately 20":

Pink—eight picks

White—four picks

Dark brown—eight picks

White—four picks

After weaving the back panel to its final length and completing the color order above, finish by weaving eight picks of pink.

Tea cozy, back panel

Weave additional front and back panels if planned. Then remove from the loom and prepare for sewing by stitching raw ends, washing in cold water, air drying, and ironing (hot iron, steam setting).

Approximate finished dimensions of one front panel (unhemmed):

**Width:** 17"

**Length:** 13½"

Approximate finished dimensions of one back panel (unhemmed):

**Width:** 16¾"

**Length:** 15¼"

## PROJECT NOTES

The three words for this project are placed separately on three different levels and will be laid in successively rather than simultaneously. As you prepare to lay in the pattern, begin by identifying the center point for the entire pattern rather than for each word individually and measure the placement of each of the three words from that point.

The bird's eye and wing are areas where no pattern is inserted, with the woven background alone providing a light highlight against the black body and head. See "Using Background Without Pattern" in chapter 2.

## TEA COZY SEWING INSTRUCTIONS

### MATERIALS:

Cotton fabric for the lining and cotton batting, each cut to approximately 12" by 15"

The handwoven front and back panel

Quilt binding material and piping

Supplies and tools:

Sewing machine with a walking foot and zipper or piping foot

Quilting thread

Pins and scissors

Cozy sewing pattern (instructions below)

Machine needles such as Schmetz size 80/12 or 90/14 Quilting, Jeans, or Microtex points

### SEWING-PATTERN INSTRUCTIONS:

Align two 8½" by 11" paper sheets on the long sides, making a rectangle that is 11" high and 16¾" wide. Tape the sheets together.

Draw a horizontal line that is 13½" in length, centered ¼" above the bottom edge of the rectangle. When centered on the sheet, the line's two ends should each be approximately 1½" from the ends of the sheet.

Draw a second horizontal line that is 6" in length, centered ¼" below the top edge of the rectangle. When centered on the sheet, the line's two ends should each be approximately 5¼" from the ends of the sheet.

The distance between the two horizontal lines will be 10½".

Connect the ends of the horizontal lines by drawing lines that extend upward vertically for 6" from the bottom line before curving inward to meet the upper horizontal line. If necessary, adjust the curving lines to fashion nicely rounded "shoulders" at either side.

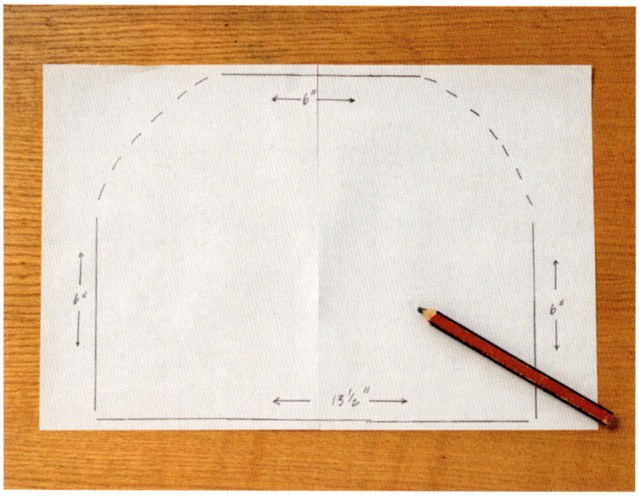

With scissors, cut along the lines you have drawn to make the pattern.

### ASSEMBLING THE TEA COZY

**Step 1.** Place the cozy sewing pattern on the right side of the front panel. Cut out and set aside.

Repeat step 1 for the back panel (placing the pattern on the bias if desired), as well as the lining and batting (two pieces each).

**Step 2.** Align the front panel over the batting, with the right side facing up, and pin. Sew the panel and batting together with a 3 mm straight stitch. (A walking foot is helpful to prevent shifting or puckering.) Press and set aside.

Repeat step 2 to assemble the tea cozy back.

**Step 3.** Place together two pieces of the lining and pin. Stitch together with a 2.5–3 mm straight stitch, leaving the bottom open. Trim any excess fabric and set aside.

**Step 4.** Pin the piping to the cozy front. Adjust the needle position to the right, then sew around the outer edge, using a 4 mm straight stitch and a zipper or piping foot.

**Step 5.** For the hanging tab, cut a 4" length of the binding material. Fold in half lengthwise and stitch along the open edge. Then stitch along the opposite edge for visual symmetry. Fold the strip in half to make a loop. Stitch the tab into place at the center back of the cozy.

**Step 6.** Align the cozy back and front together, with the wrong sides facing outward, and pin. Adjust the needle position slightly to the left and sew the back and front together along the curved edge, using a 3 mm straight stitch and a zipper or piping foot. Leave the bottom open. Trim any excess fabric remaining at the curves. Turn the cozy right side out and press.

**Step 7.** Insert the lining into the cozy and trim any excess lining left at the bottom. Pin the lining to the raw edge at the bottom of the cozy. Using a walking foot, stitch the layers together around the bottom edge.

**Step 8.** For the bottom edge binding, place a length of binding material around the bottom edge of the cozy. Cut the material where the two ends meet, folding back a ½" hem at either end. Align the two folded edges together and join them securely with a pin. Remove the strip from the cozy, open the two hems just created, and, working on the wrong side, sew the ends together along the fold line of the hems.

**Step 9.** Mark the center back and center front at the bottom edge of the cozy. Mark the center of the binding and align that center mark with the center front. Beginning at that mark, fold the binding around the bottom edge of the cozy, turning from the outside to the inside, and pin. Continue folding the binding around the cozy bottom, securing it with pins as you work. Then stitch the binding to the cozy, using a 3 mm straight stitch. Trim any excess threads and press.

Neptune
old-as-time
diver
N
E
S

# MARINER'S COMPASS

*Project:*
## PILLOW

### PREPARATION

Dimensions are based on a pillow insert that is 16" square.

**Weave structure:** plain weave

**Warp:** 40/2 linen in natural, 6,000 yards per pound

**Weft:** 40/2 linen in white, 6,000 yards per pound

**Sett:** 32 ends per inch

**Number of warp ends:** 640

**Width in the reed:** 20"

**Warp length:** Wind a 3-yard warp in natural linen for one pillow front panel and one back panel plus extra for loom waste. In total, 3,840 yards of linen (10½ oz. by weight) will be required for warp and weft combined (excluding the linen used for the pattern).

**Loom preparation:** Dress and treadle for plain weave

**Pattern colors/yardage for one front panel using 40/2 linen** (allowing for doubled strands and waste): blue (175 yards)

### WEAVING THE PROJECT AND LAYING IN THE PATTERN

Review the General Instructions for the Projects.

The pattern is 114 columns wide (equaling 114 raised warp ends), with the center of the pattern found at the vertical line between the 57th and 58th columns. Use white linen for the background weft. Begin the front panel by weaving a header, 7" in length. Continue by laying in the pattern, centered in the warp. After laying in, the pattern itself will be approximately 8" in length. Finish by weaving to a total length of 22".

Weave the back panel to a length of 22", using white or blue linen for the weft. You will need approximately 550 yards (1½ oz.) of linen for the weft for the back panel. Then remove from the loom and prepare for sewing by stitching raw ends, washing in cold water, air drying, and ironing (hot iron, steam setting).

Neptune and Mariner's Compass pillows, back panels, woven in blue

Approximate finished dimensions of one front panel (unhemmed):

**Width:** 18½"

**Length:** 20½"

Approximate finished dimensions of one back panel (unhemmed):

**Width:** 18½"

**Length:** 20½"

## PILLOW SEWING INSTRUCTIONS

### WHEN USING PIPING:

**Step 1.** Pin the piping to the right side of the front pillow panel, with the raw edges of the piping and the front panel together. As you pin, follow the dotted lines shown on the Pillow Stitching Guide, taking care to taper the pillow's four corners. Clip the piping seam allowance so that it bends at the corners. The seam allowance should be approximately ½" from the raw edges on the sides, and ¾" at the corners. The "join" of the piping should be at the center bottom of the pillow.

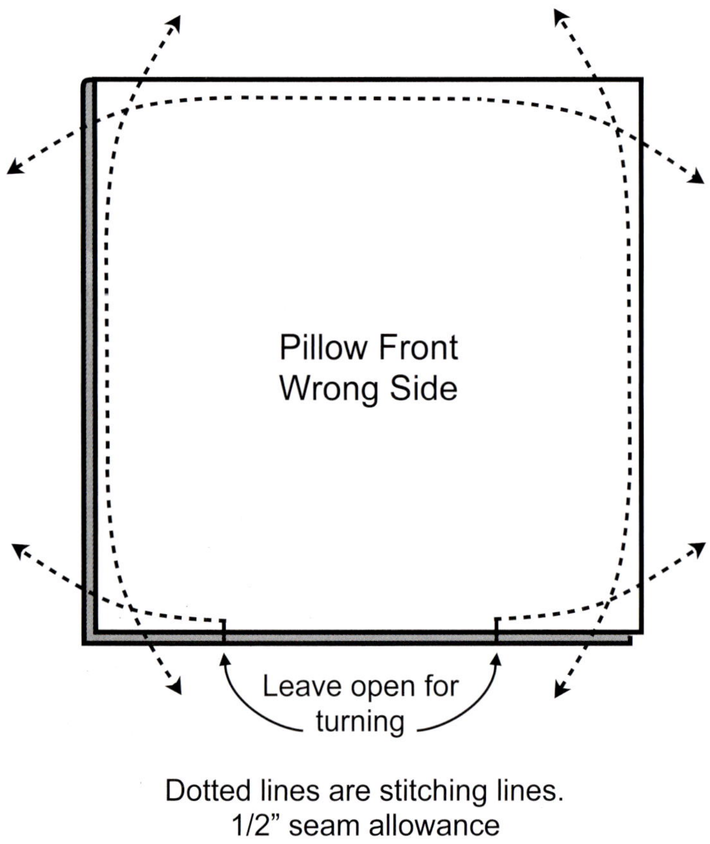


Pillow Stitching Guide

**Step 2.** Attach a zipper foot to the sewing machine and adjust the needle position to the left. Use a 4–5 mm straight stitch to sew the piping to the front panel, working close to the piping "bump."

**Step 3.** With the right sides together, align the rear pillow panel on the front panel and pin.

**Step 4.** Use a 3 mm straight stitch to join the two panels together, working close to the piping, leaving a section of the bottom open, as shown on the Pillow Stitching Guide. Trim any excess fabric at the corners.

**Step 5.** Turn the pillow right side out and press. Stuff the pillow with a premade pillow form or poly stuffing.

**Step 6.** Close the opening at the bottom with hand stitching.

### WHEN NOT USING PIPING:

**Step 1.** Attach a walking foot to the sewing machine. Then align the pillow front and rear panels with the right sides together and pin.

**Step 2.** Use a 3 mm straight stitch to join the two pillow panels together. The seam allowance should be approximately ½" on the sides, and ¾" at the corners. Leave a section of the bottom open to turn the pillow right side out, as shown on the Pillow Stitching Guide. Trim any excess fabric at the corners.

**Step 3.** Turn the pillow right side out and press. Stuff the pillow with a premade pillow form or new poly stuffing.

**Step 4.** Close the opening at the bottom with hand stitching.

# NEPTUNE

## *Project:* PILLOW

### PREPARATION

Dimensions are based on a pillow insert that is 20" by 26".

**Weave structure:** plain weave

**Warp:** 40/2 linen in natural, 6,000 yards per pound

**Weft:** 40/2 linen in white, 6,000 yards per pound

**Sett:** 32 ends per inch

**Number of warp ends:** 801

**Width in the reed:** 25"

**Warp length:** Wind a 4-yard warp in natural linen for one pillow front panel and one back panel plus extra for loom waste. In total, 6,400 yards of linen (1 lb., 1 oz. by weight) will be required for warp and weft combined (excluding the linen used for the pattern).

**Loom preparation:** Dress and treadle for plain weave

**Pattern colors/yardage for one front panel using 40/2 linen (allowing for doubled strands and waste):** blue (300 yards)

### WEAVING THE PROJECT AND LAYING IN THE PATTERN

Review the General Instructions for the Projects.

The pattern is 223 columns wide (equaling 223 raised warp ends), with the center of the pattern found at the 112th column. Use white linen for the background weft. Begin the front panel by weaving a header, 5" in length. Continue by laying in the pattern, centered in the warp. After laying in, the pattern itself will be approximately 23" in length (measured to the top of the trident). Finish by weaving to a total length of 33".

Weave the back panel to a length of 33", using white or blue linen for the weft. You will need approximately 750 yards (2 oz.) of linen for the weft for the back panel. Then remove from the loom and prepare for sewing by stitching raw ends, washing in cold water, air drying, and ironing (hot iron, steam setting).

Approximate finished dimensions of one front panel (unhemmed):

**Width:** 23"

**Length:** 31"

Approximate finished dimensions of one back panel (unhemmed):

**Width:** 23"

**Length:** 31"

To assemble the pillow, refer to the Pillow Sewing Instructions

# STAR-OF-THE-MEADOW*

*Project:*
## NAPKINS

### PREPARATION

**Weave structure:** plain weave

**Warp and weft:** 40/2 linen in white, 6,000 yards per pound

**Sett:** 32 ends per inch

**Number of warp ends:** 576

**Width in the reed:** 18"

**Warp length:** Wind a 4-yard warp in white linen for four napkins plus extra for sampling and loom waste. In total, 4,608 yards of linen (12½ oz. by weight) will be required for warp and weft combined (excluding the linen used for the pattern).

**For eight napkins, wind a 6-yard warp:** 6,912 yards (1 lb., 3 oz. by weight)

**Loom preparation:** Dress and treadle for plain weave

**Pattern colors/yardage for each napkin using 40/2 linen, accounting for a single napkin woven in each of four color combinations (allowing for doubled strands and waste):**

- Napkin with pink flower: pink (15 yards), blue (5 yards), green (15 yards)
- Napkin with blue flower: blue (15 yards), pink (5 yards), green (15 yards)
- Napkin with yellow flower: yellow (15 yards), blue (5 yards), pink (10 yards), green (15 yards)
- Napkin with green flower: light green, petals (15 yards), blue (15 yards), green, stems and leaves (15 yards)

**Star-of-the-meadow is an imaginary wildflower.*

### WEAVING THE PROJECT AND LAYING IN THE PATTERN

Review the General Instructions for the Projects.

The draft for this project includes four individual color possibilities. The pattern for each individual flower is 30 columns wide (equaling 30 raised warp ends), with the center of the pattern found at the vertical line between the 15th and 16th columns. Use white linen for the background weft. Begin each napkin by weaving a header, 2" in length. Continue by laying in the pattern, consisting of a single flower, centered in the warp. After laying in, the pattern itself will be approximately 3½" in length. Finish by weaving to a total length of 20".

Weave additional napkins if planned. Then remove from the loom and finish by stitching raw ends, washing in cold water, air drying, ironing (hot iron, steam setting), and hemming.

Approximate finished dimensions of one napkin after hemming:

**Width:** 17½"

**Length:** 16½"

Star-of-the-meadow

# STAR-OF-THE-MEADOW

*Project:*
## DISH TOWEL

### PREPARATION

**Weave structure:** plain weave

**Warp and weft:** 40/2 linen in white, 6,000 yards per pound

**Sett:** 32 ends per inch

**Number of warp ends:** 641

**Width in the reed:** 20"

**Warp length:** Wind a 3-yard warp in white linen for one dish towel plus extra for sampling and loom waste. When weaving multiple dish towels, add an extra yard to the warp (requiring an additional 1,280 yards for warp and weft combined) for each additional towel as follows:

**3-yard warp, one towel:** 3,840 yards in total for warp and weft, 10½ oz. by weight (excluding the linen used for the pattern)

**4-yard warp, two towels:** 5,120 yards (13½ oz. by weight)

**5-yard warp, three towels:** 6,400 yards (1 lb. 1 oz. by weight)

**Loom preparation:** Dress and treadle for plain weave

**Pattern colors/yardage for one dish towel using 40/2 linen (allowing for doubled strands and waste):** pink (15 yards), medium brown (30 yards), blue (5 yards), green (15 yards)

### WEAVING THE PROJECT AND LAYING IN THE PATTERN

Review the General Instructions for the Projects.

The pattern is 163 columns wide (equaling 163 raised warp ends), with the center of the pattern at the 82nd column. Use white linen for the background weft. Begin each dish towel by weaving a header, 3" in length. Continue by laying in the pattern, centered in the warp. After laying in, the pattern be approximately 3½" in length. Finish by weaving to a total length of 30".

Weave additional dish towels if planned. Then remove from the loom and finish by stitching raw ends, washing in cold water, air drying, ironing (hot iron, steam setting), and hemming.

Approximate finished dimensions of one dish towel after hemming:

**Width:** 18½"

**Length:** 25½"

Star-of-the-meadow

# STAR-OF-THE-MEADOW

*Project:*
## PLACEMATS

### PREPARATION

**Weave structure:** plain weave

**Warp and weft:** 40/2 linen in white, 6,000 yards per pound

**Sett:** 32 ends per inch

**Number of warp ends:** 737

**Width in the reed:** 23"

**Warp length:** Wind a 4-yard warp in white linen for four placemats plus extra for sampling, an additional placemat if desired, and loom waste. In total, 5,888 yards of linen (16 oz. by weight) will be required for warp and weft combined (excluding the linen used for the pattern)

**Loom preparation:** Dress and treadle for plain weave

**Pattern colors/yardage for four placemats using 40/2 linen (allowing for doubled strands and waste):** pink (280 yards), medium brown (120 yards), blue (280 yards), yellow (120 yards), green (780 yards)

### WEAVING THE PROJECT AND LAYING IN THE PATTERN

Review the General Instructions for the Projects.

The pattern is 253 columns wide (equaling 253 raised warp ends), with the center of the pattern at the 127th column. Use white linen for the background weft. Begin each placemat by weaving a header, 3" in length. Continue by laying in the pattern, centered in the warp. After laying in, the pattern itself will be approximately 13" in length. Finish by weaving to a total length of 19".

Weave additional placemats if planned. Then remove from the loom and finish by stitching raw ends, washing in cold water, air drying, ironing (hot iron, steam setting), and hemming.

Approximate finished dimensions of one placemat after hemming:

**Width:** 21"

**Length:** 15"

OPPOSITE:
Plates and cup by Michael McCarthy;
bowl by Connie Talbot, High Hollow Pottery

# PROJECT DRAFTS

# BEGINNING

See project notes and instructions beginning on page 75.

155

The center is column #78

# TOGETHER

See project notes and instructions beginning on page 77.

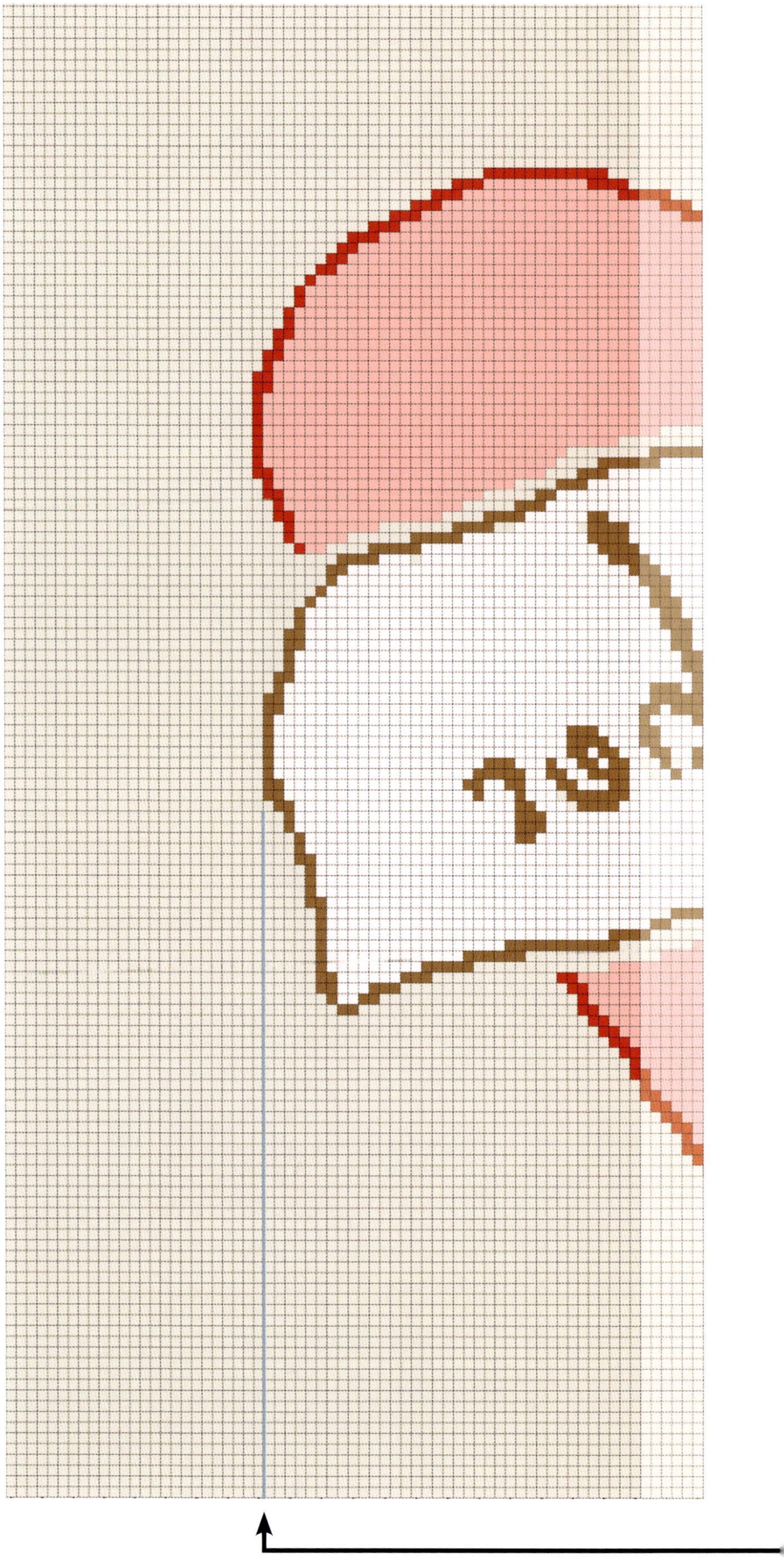

108

The center is the line between columns #54 and #55

# BIRD LOVER'S TEATIME NAPKINS

See project notes and instructions beginning on page 79.

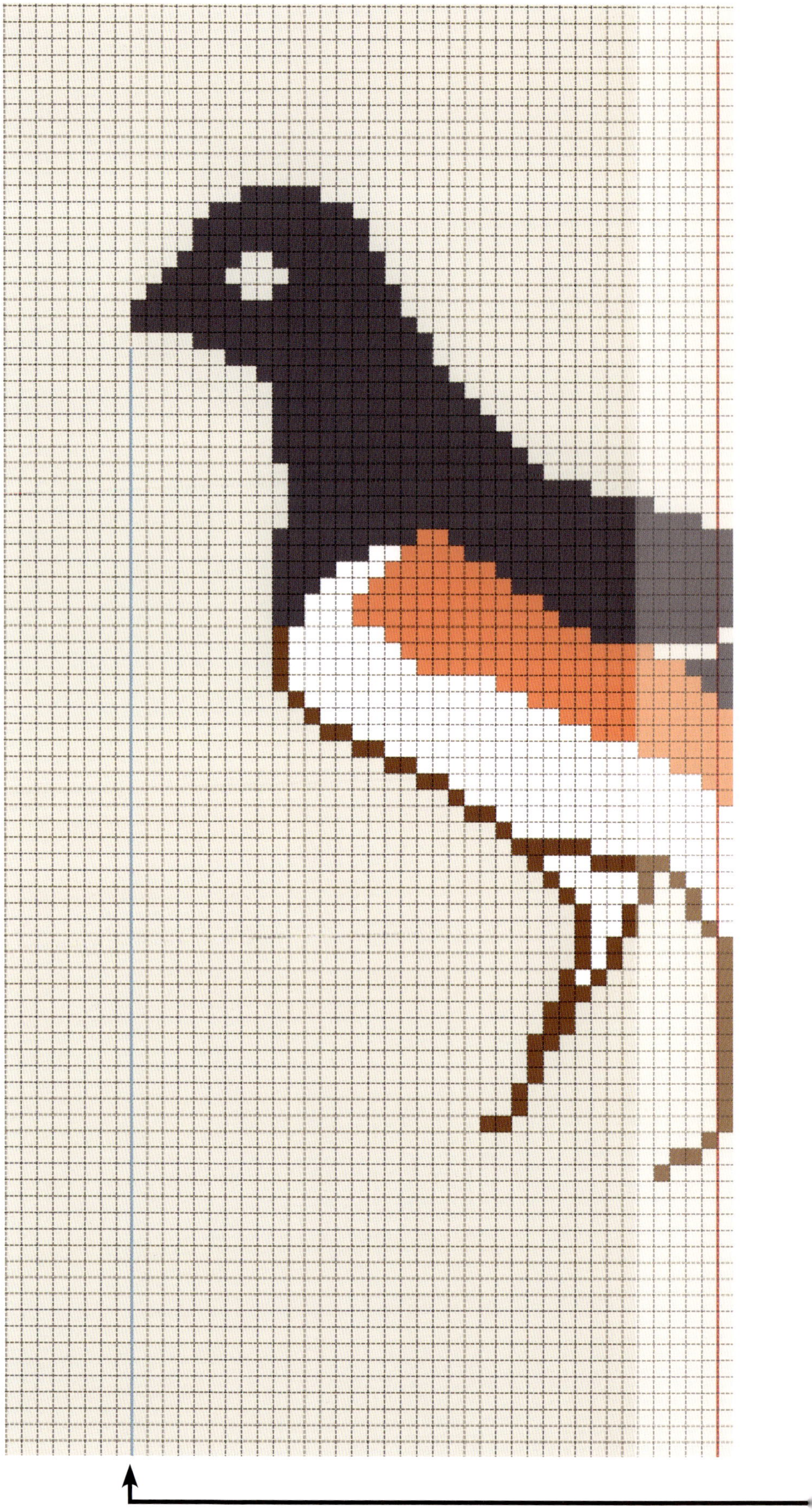

74

The center is the line between columns #37 and #38

# BIRD LOVER'S TEATIME TEA COZY

See project notes and instructions beginning on page 81.

The center is the line between columns #88 and #89

# MARINER'S COMPASS

See project notes and instructions beginning on page 85.

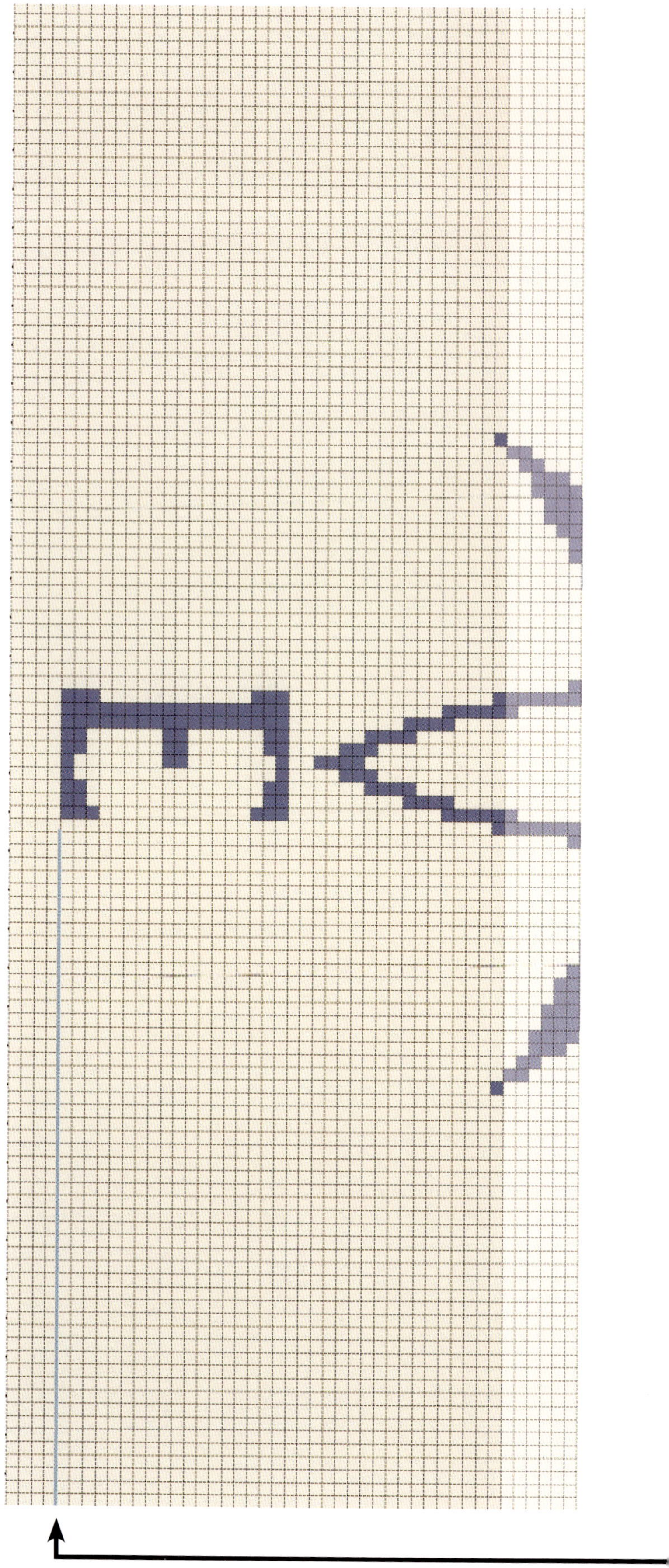

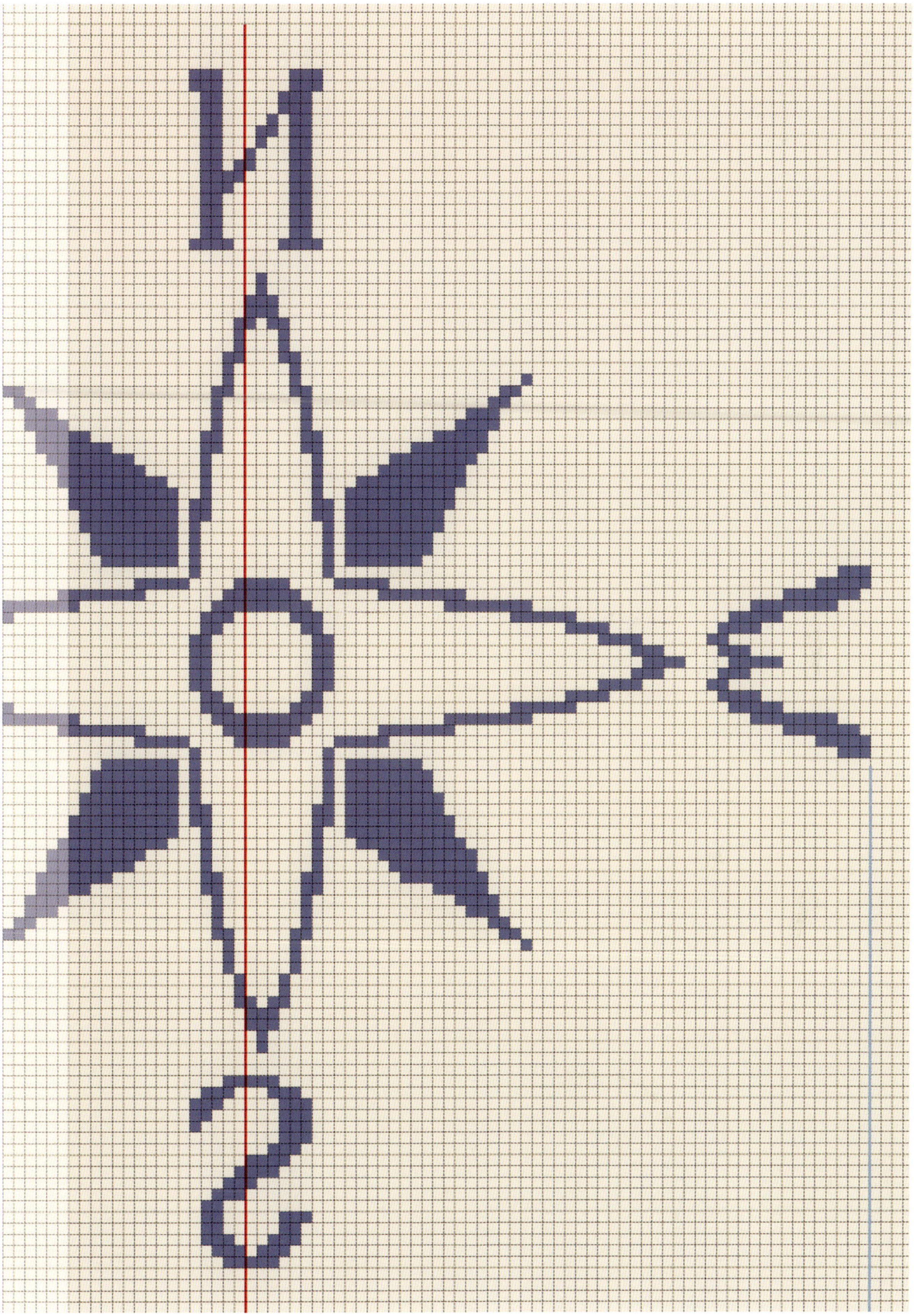

114

The center is the line between columns #57 and #58

# NEPTUNE

See project notes and instructions beginning on page 87.

223

The center is column #112

## NEPTUNE

See project notes and instructions beginning on page 87.

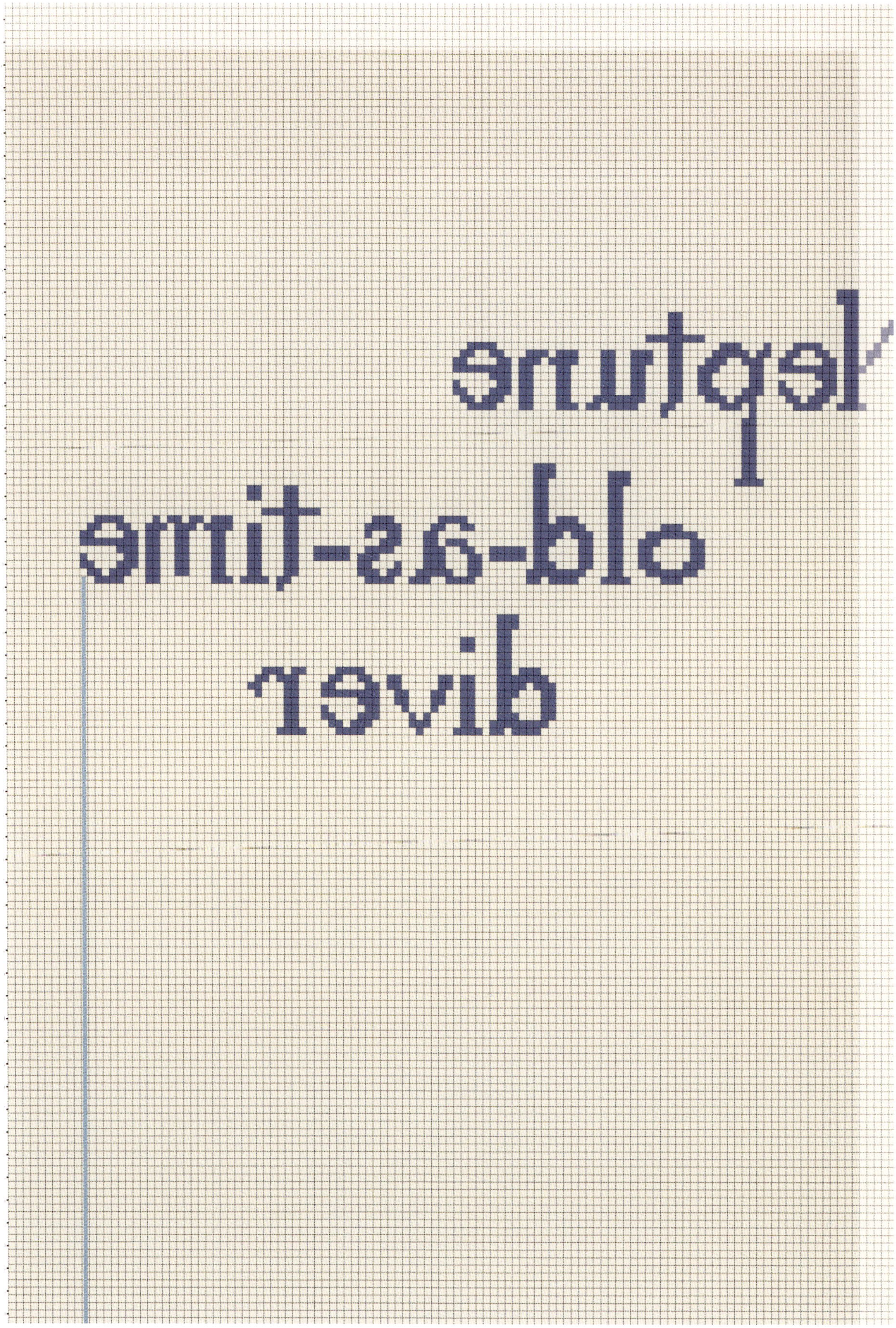

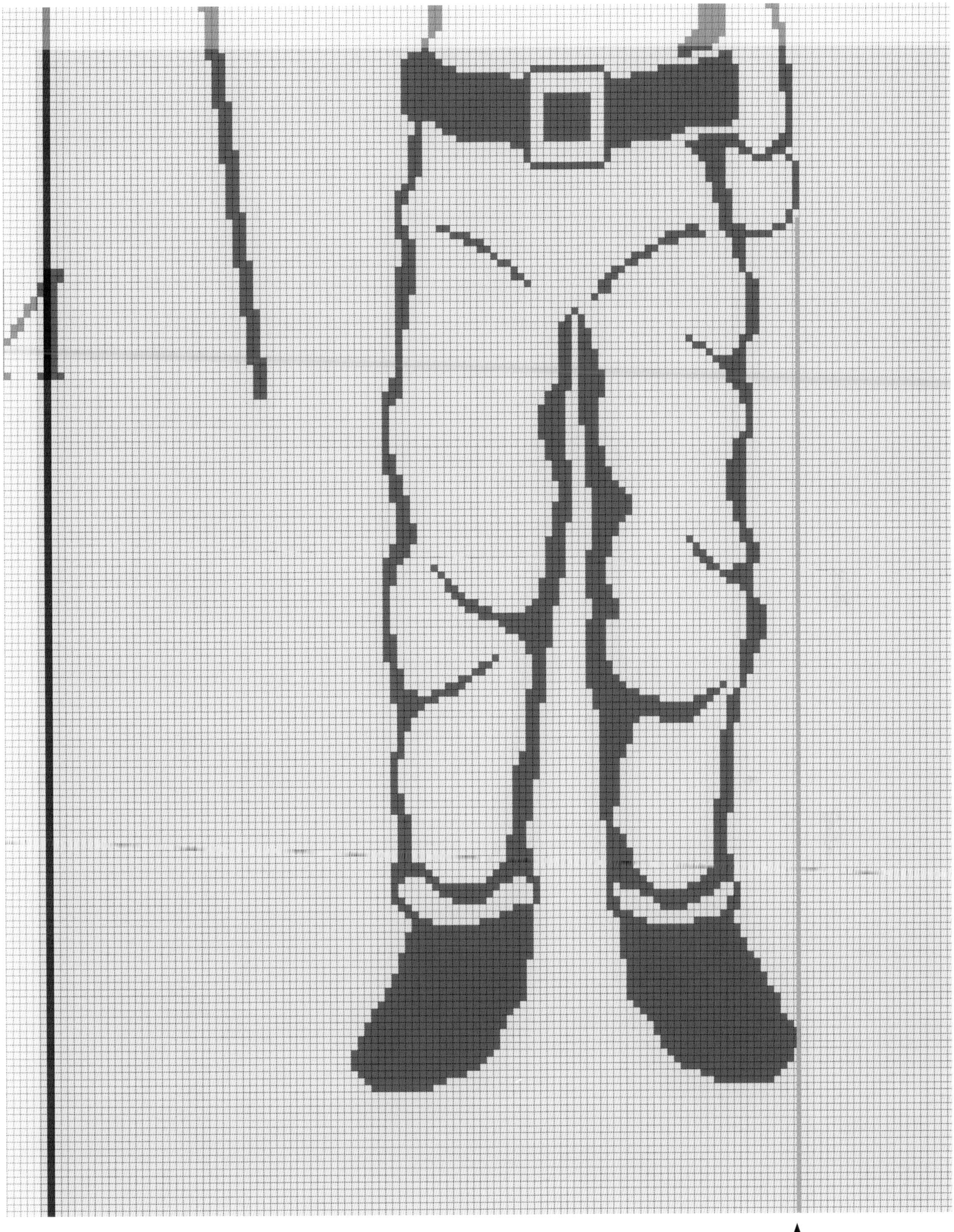

223

The center is column #112

# STAR-OF-THE-MEADOW NAPKINS

See project notes and instructions beginning on page 89.

For each pattern the center is the line between columns #15 and #16

For each pattern the center is the line between columns #15 and #16

# STAR-OF-THE-MEADOW DISH TOWEL

See project notes and instructions beginning on page 91.

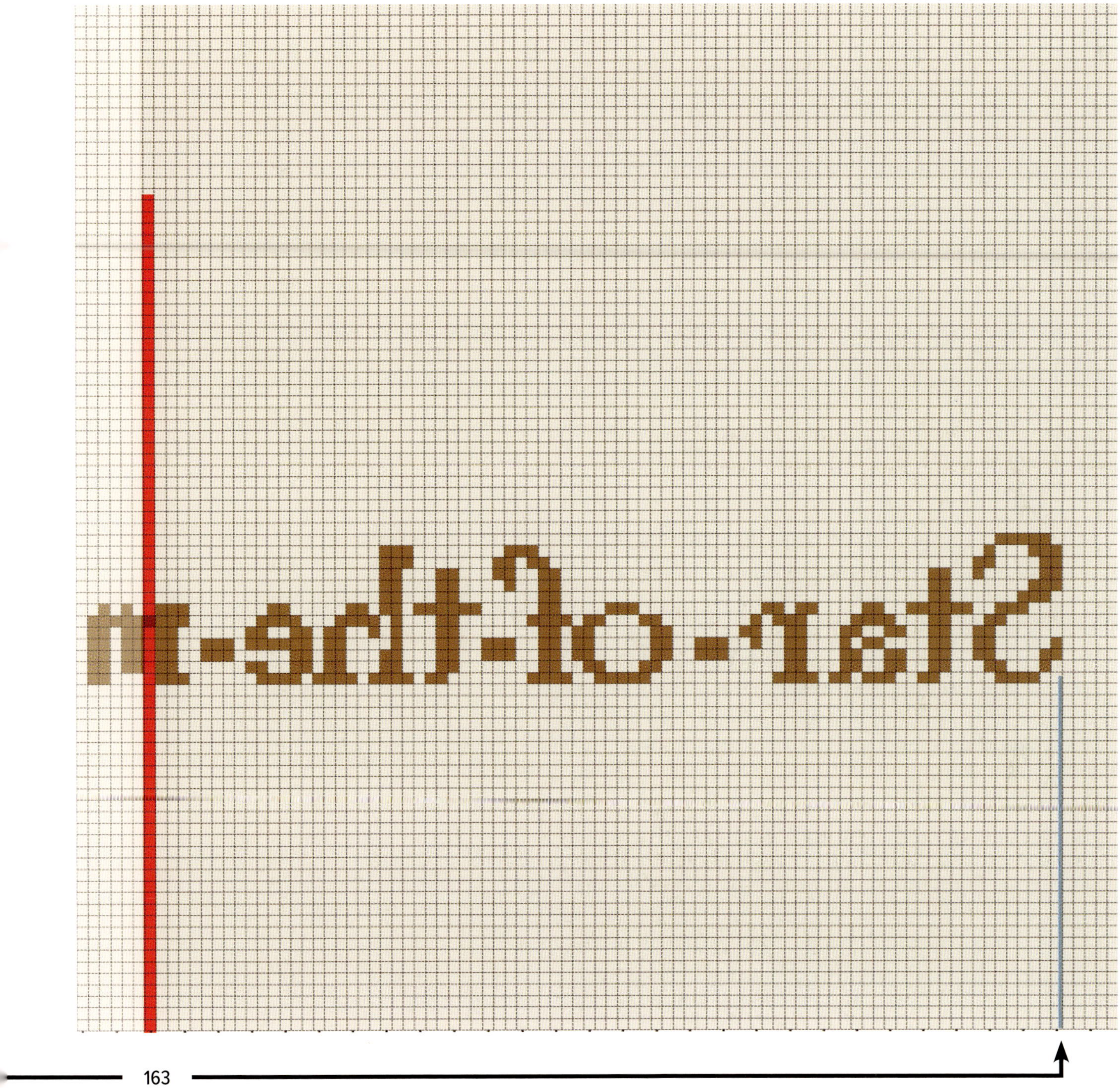


The center is column #82

# STAR-OF-THE-MEADOW PLACEMATS

See project notes and instructions beginning on page 93.

253

The center is column #127

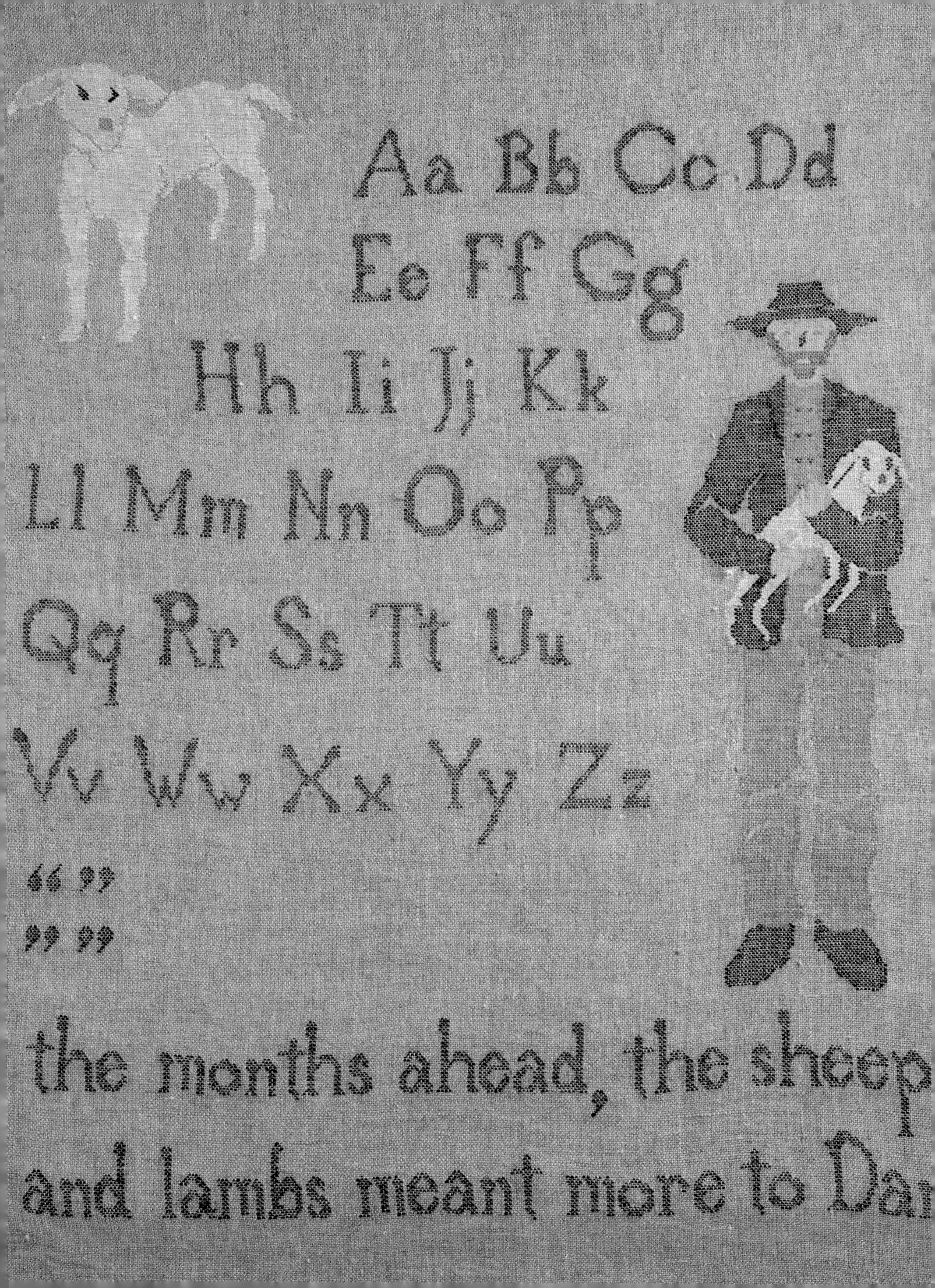
Aa Bb Cc Dd
Ee Ff Gg
Hh Ii Jj Kk
Ll Mm Nn Oo Pp
Qq Rr Ss Tt Uu
Vv Ww Xx Yy Zz
“ ”
” ”
the months ahead, the sheep
and lambs meant more to Da

*— Appendix 1 —*

# ROMAN-STYLE ALPHABET GRIDS

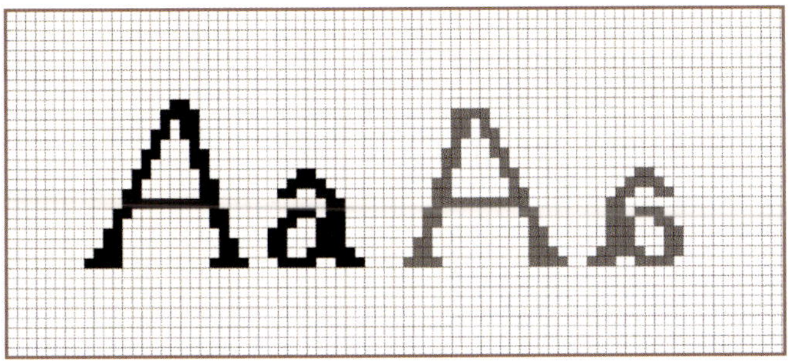

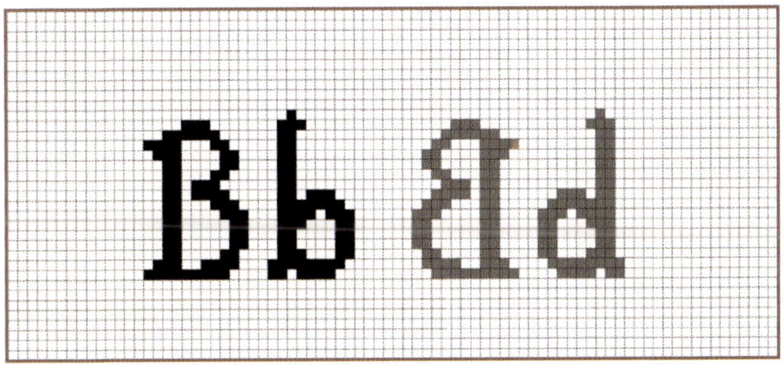

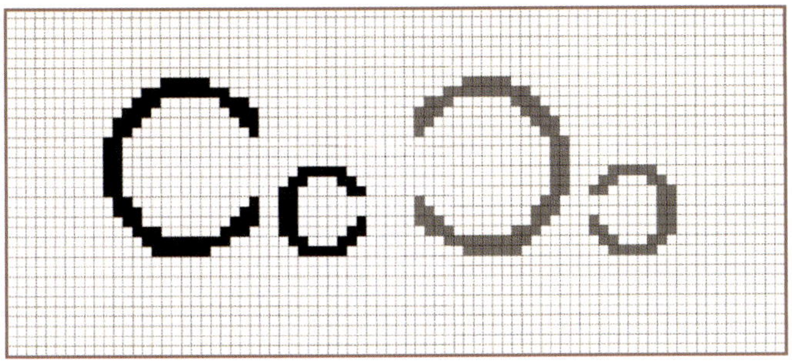

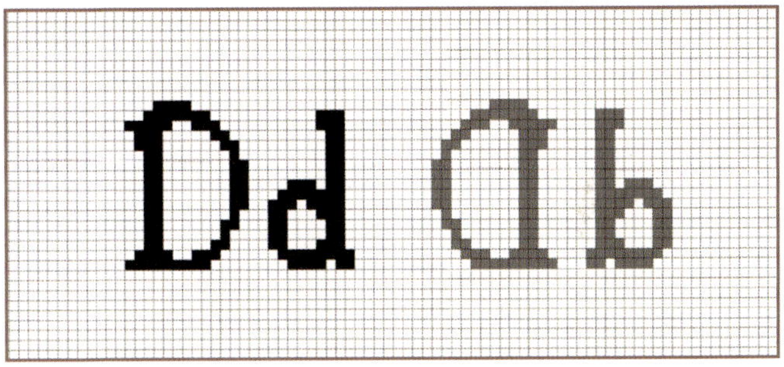

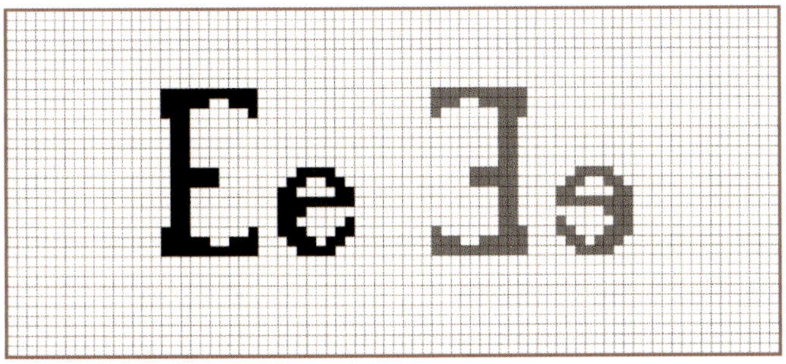

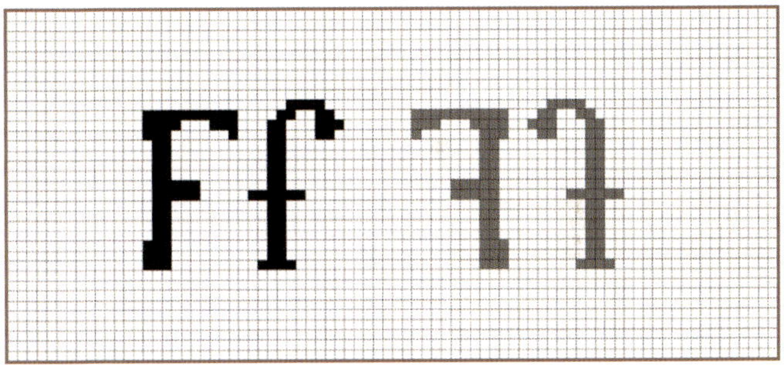

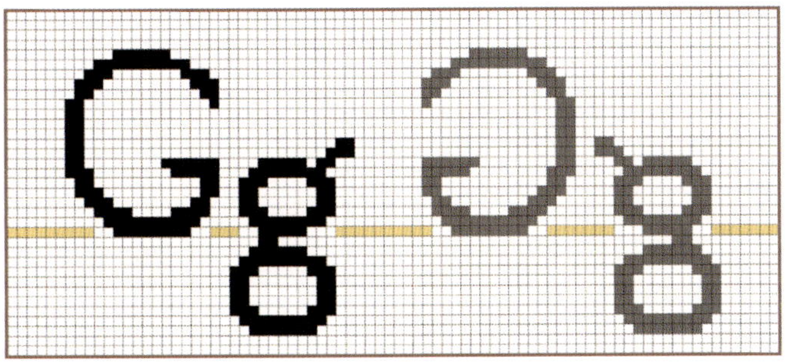

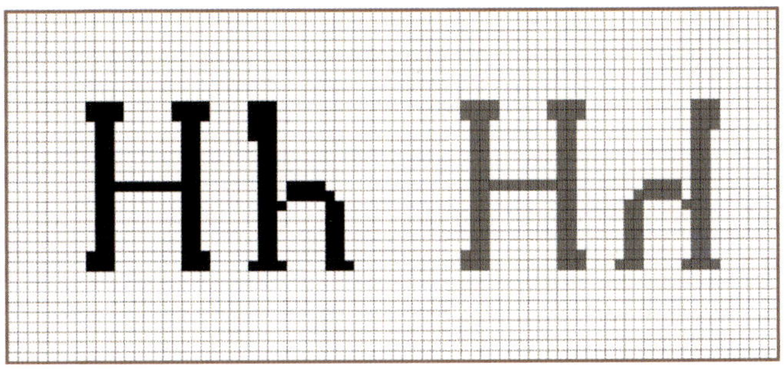

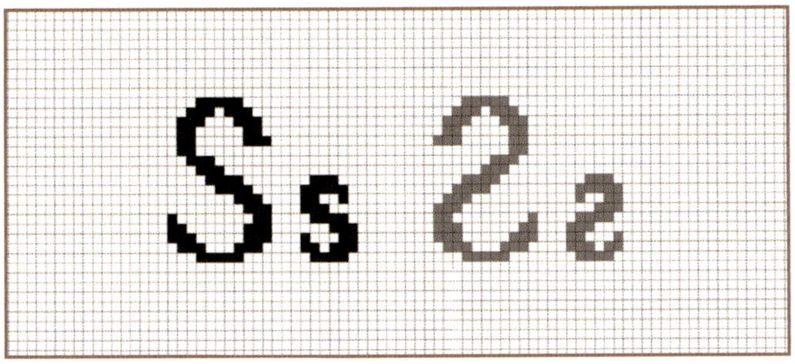
Ss Ss

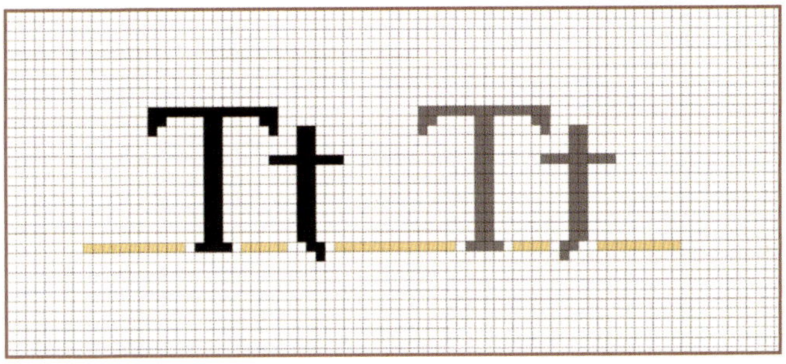
Tt Tt

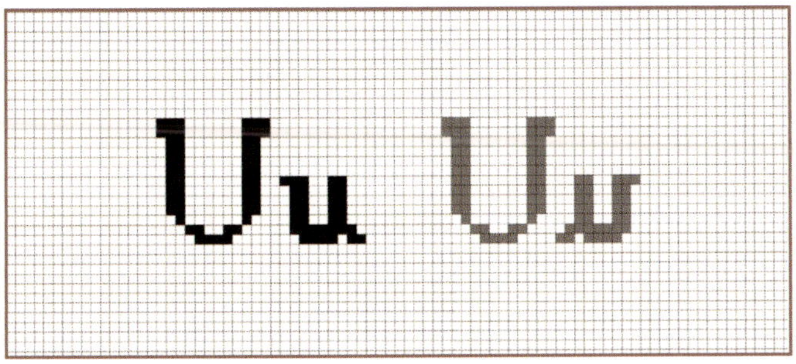
Uu Uu

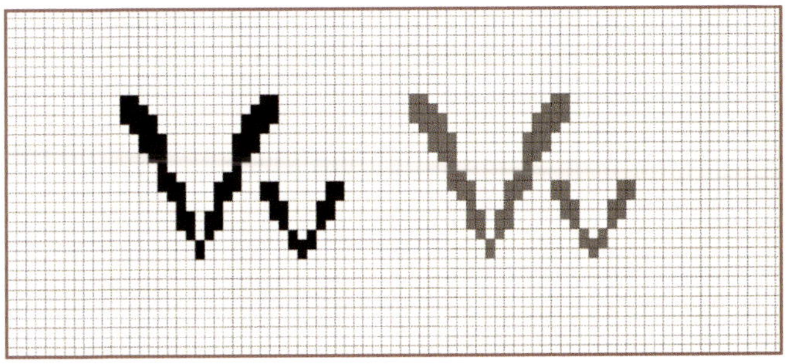
Vv Vv

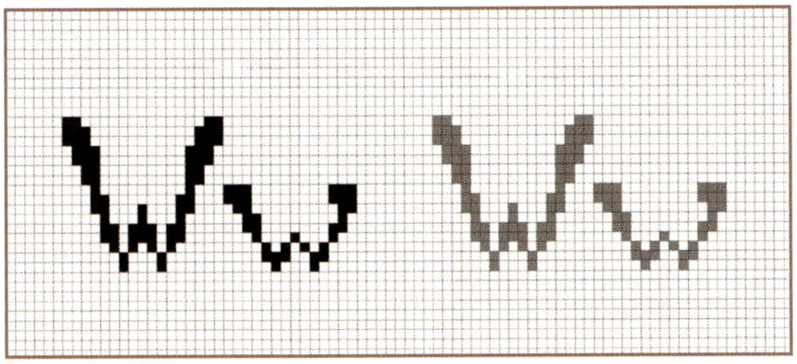
Ww Ww

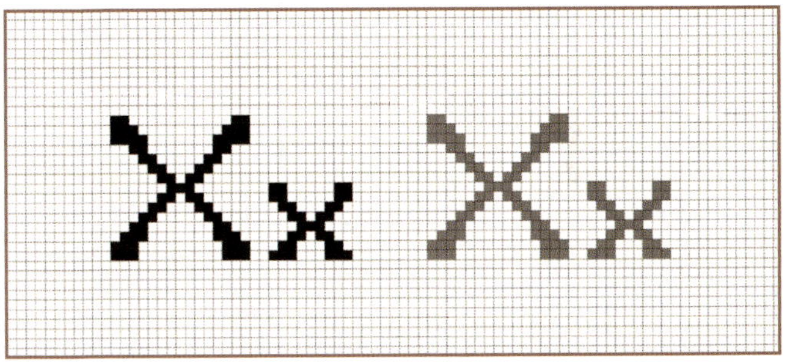
Xx Xx

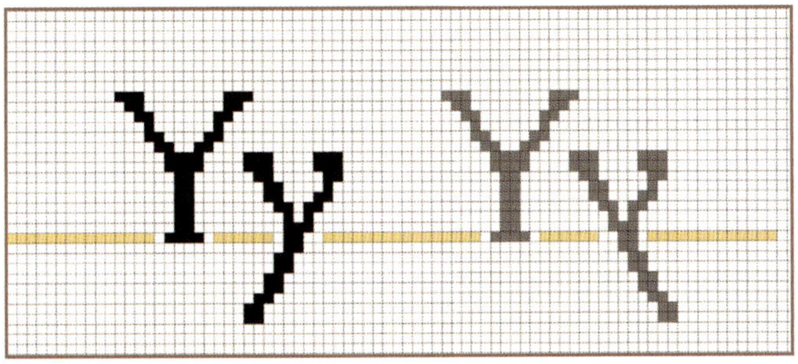
Yy Yy

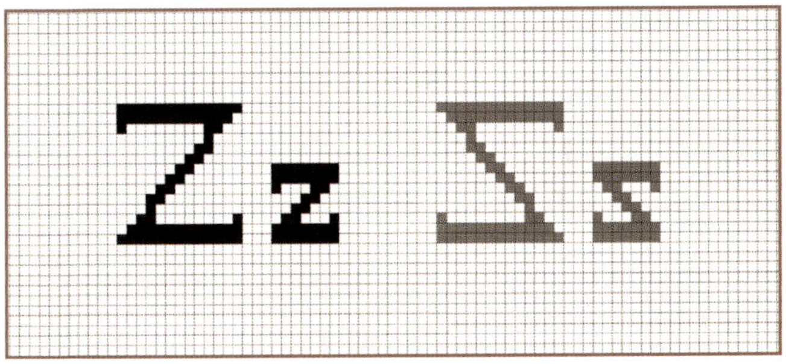
Zz Zz

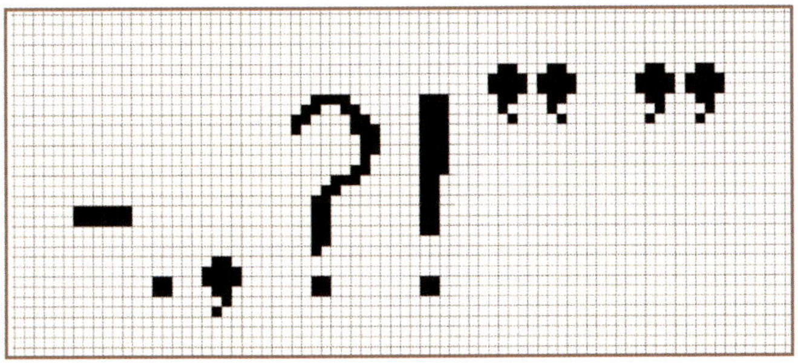
-.,?!" "

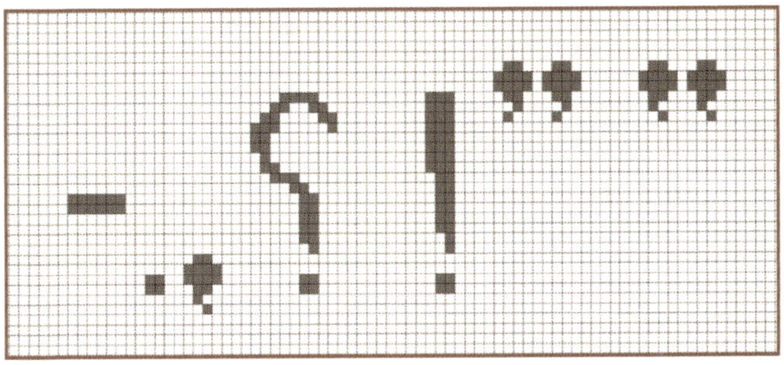
-.,?!" "

*— Appendix 2 —*

# SCRIPT-STYLE ALPHABET GRIDS

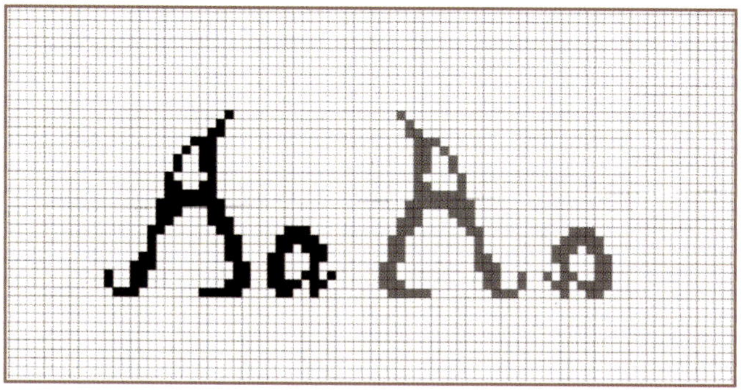

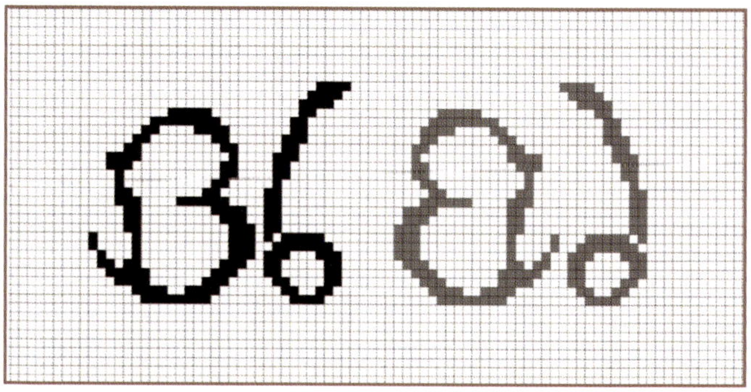

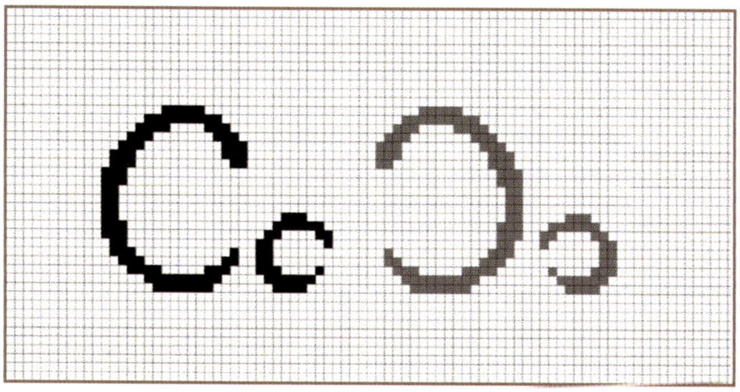

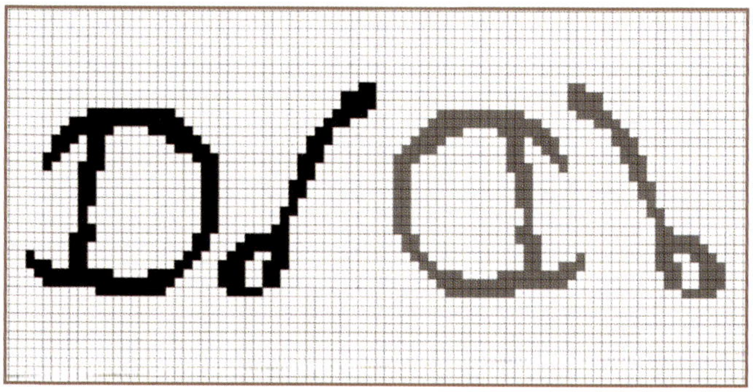

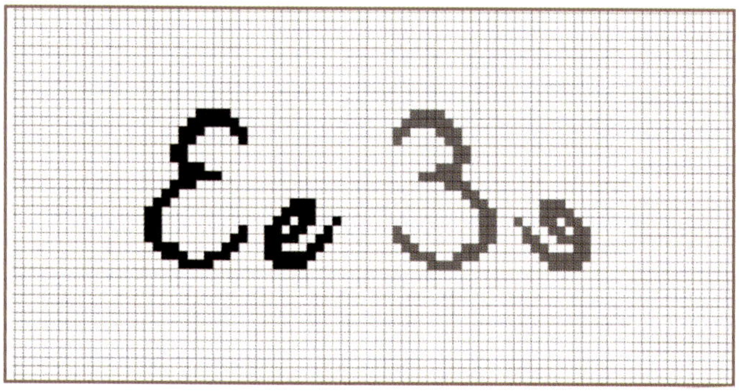

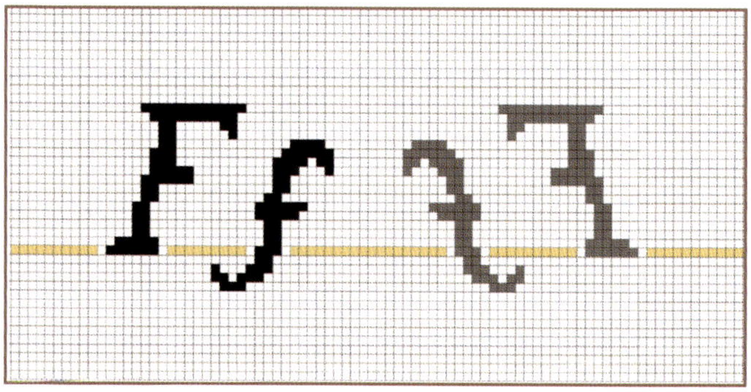

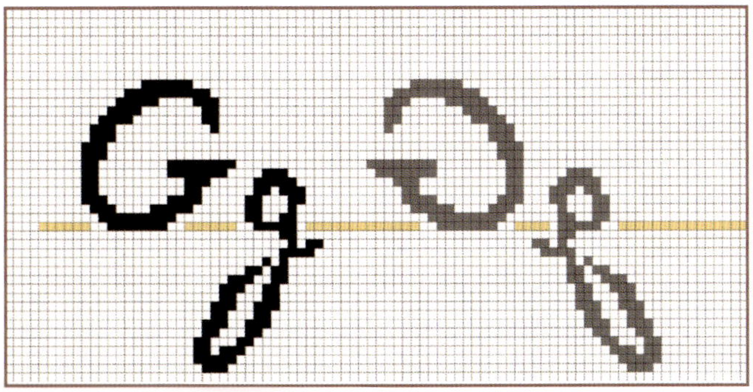

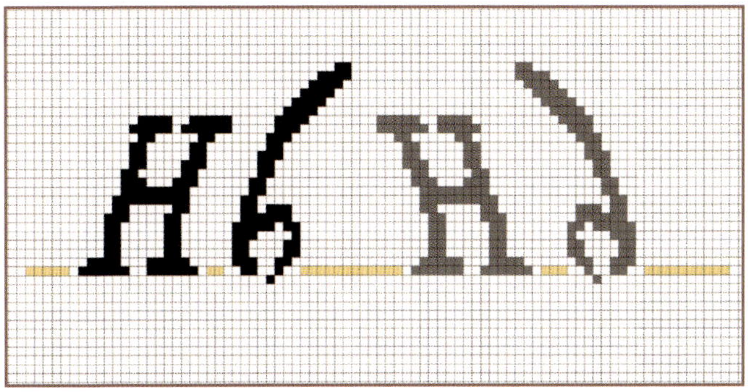

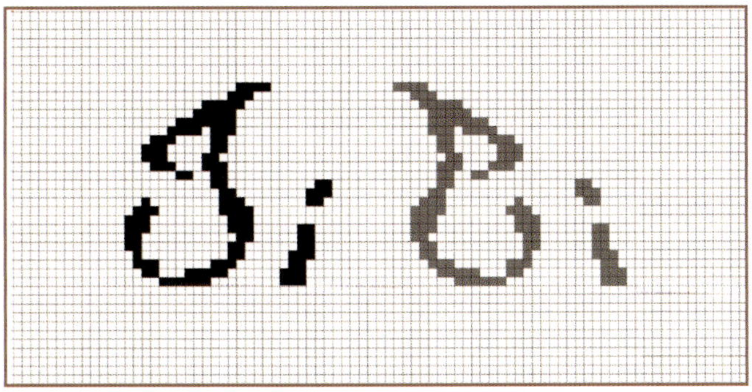

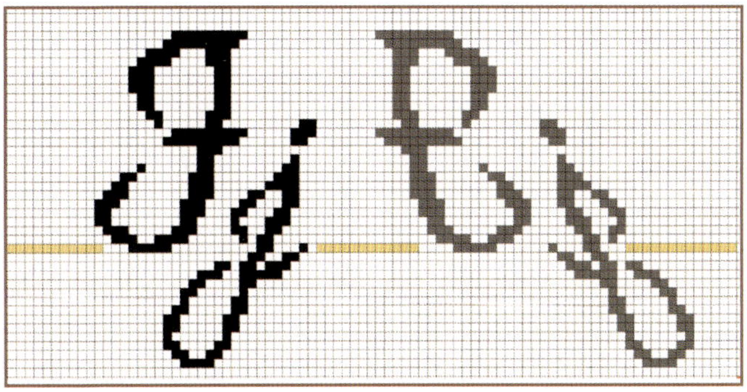

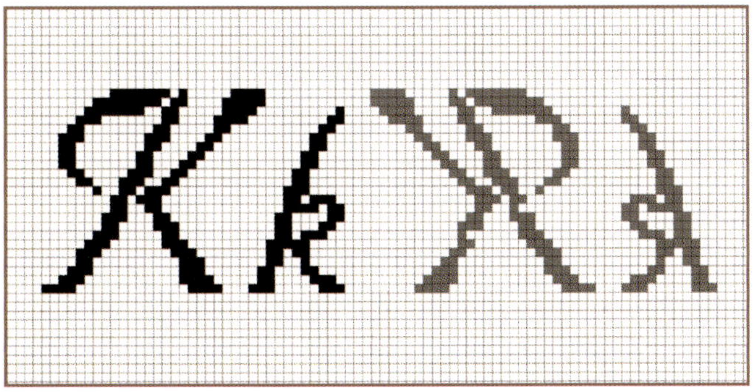

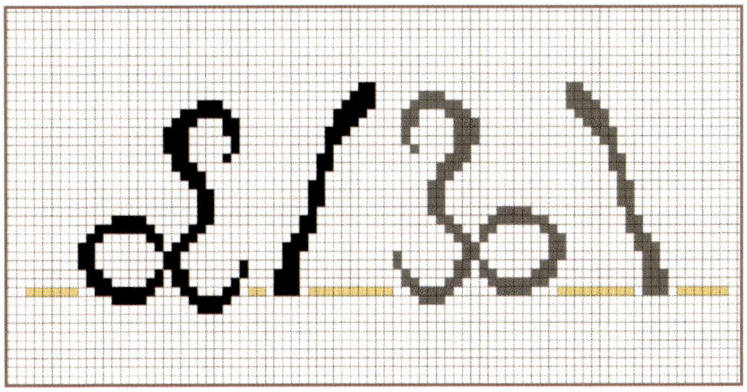

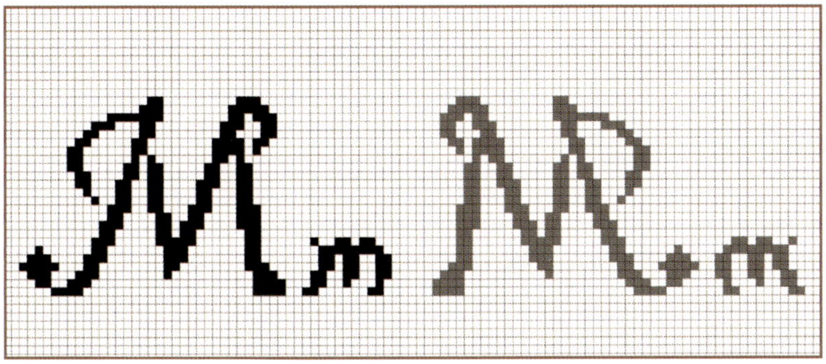

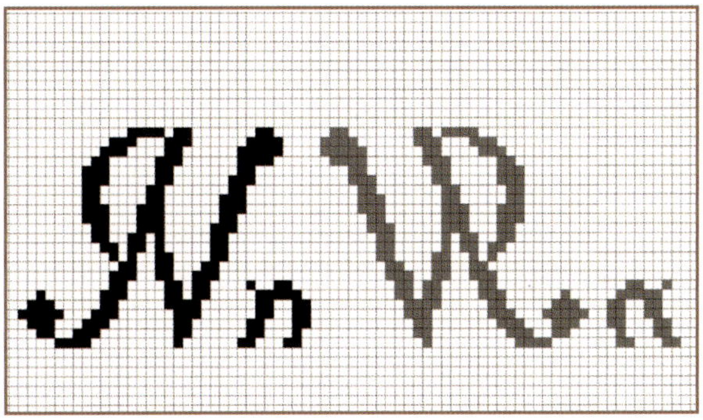

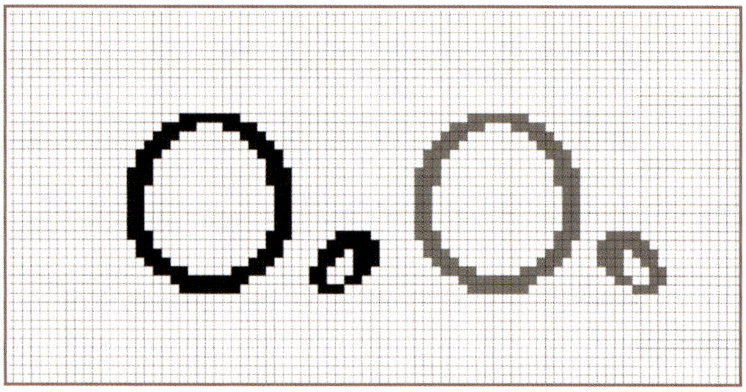
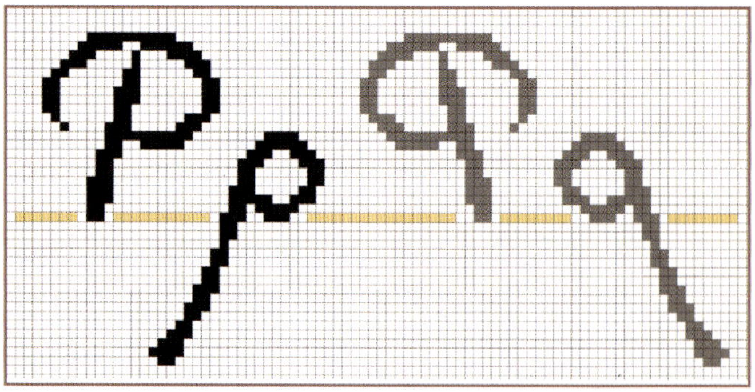
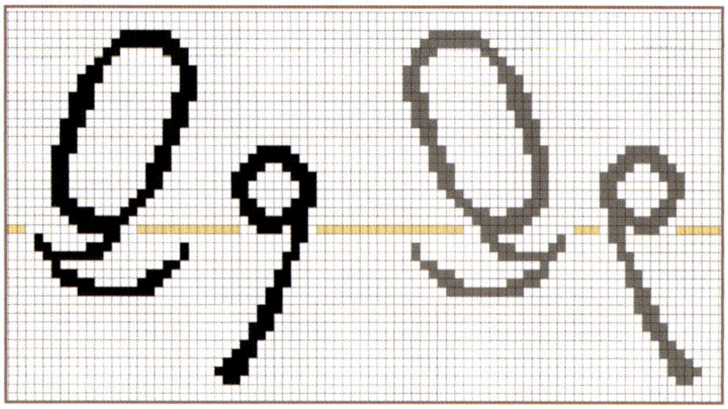
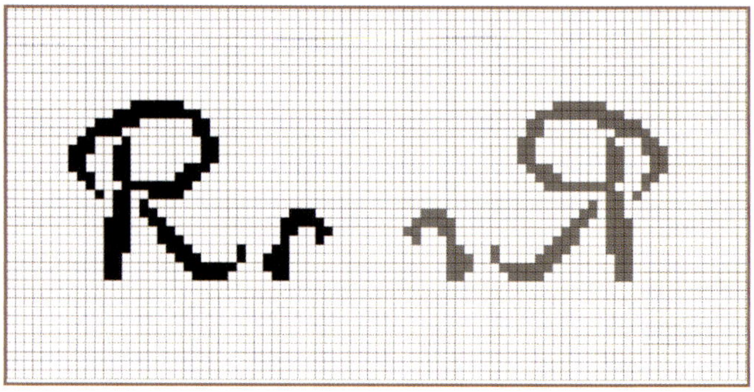
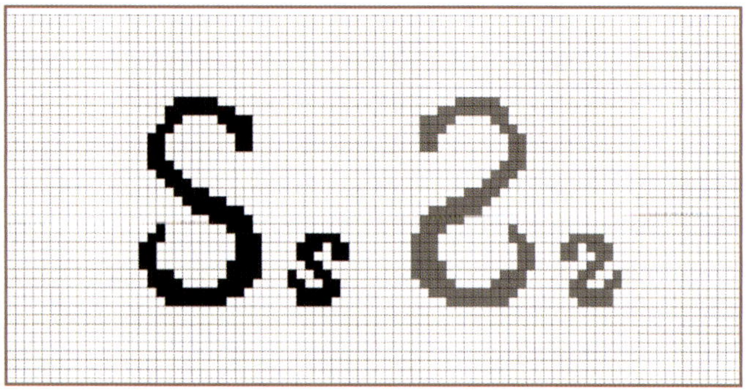
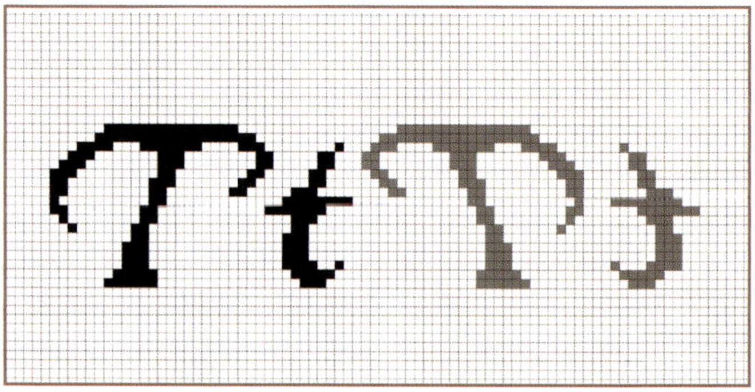
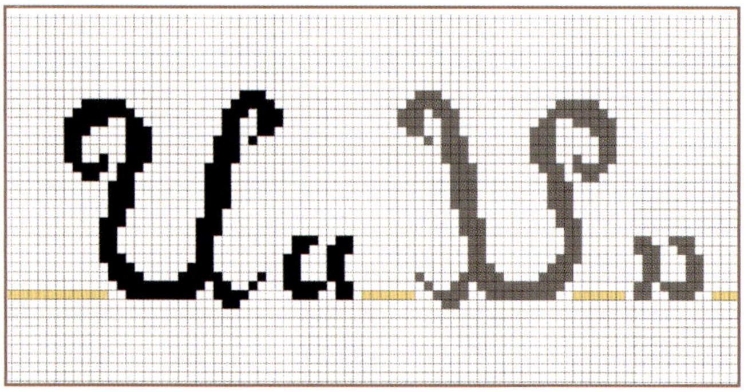
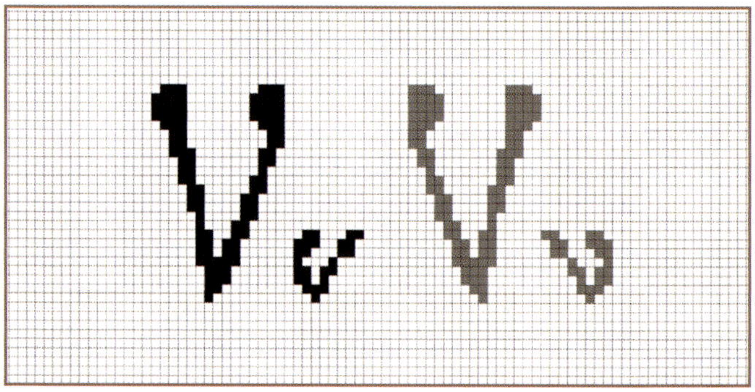

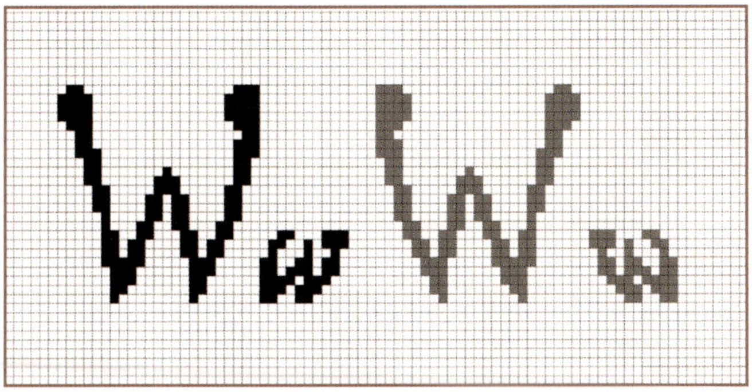

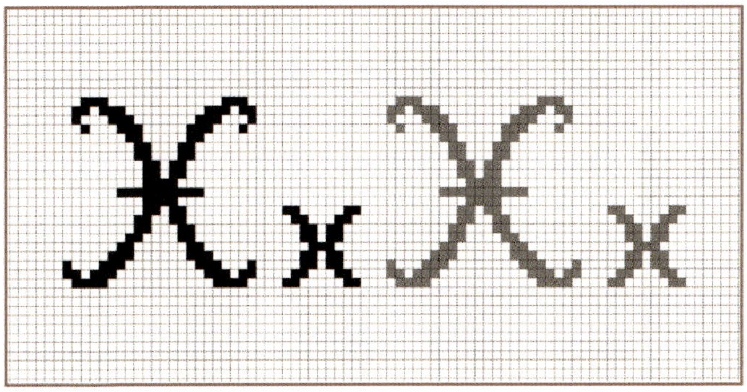

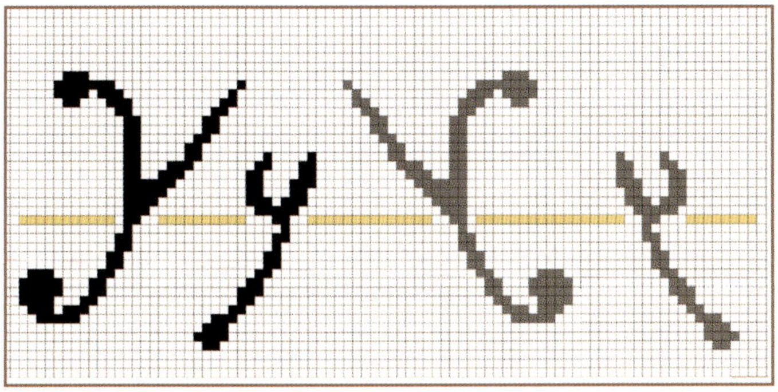

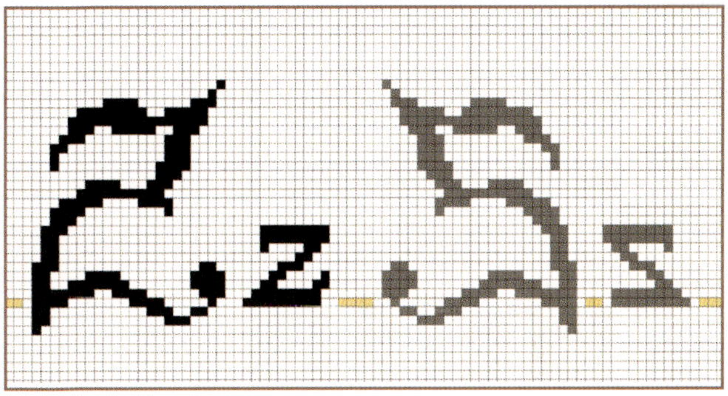

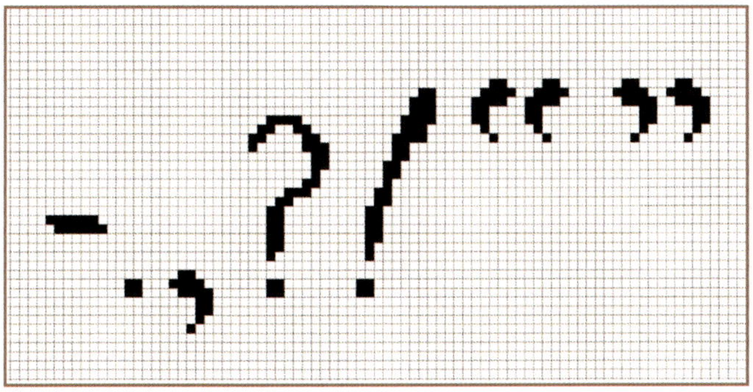

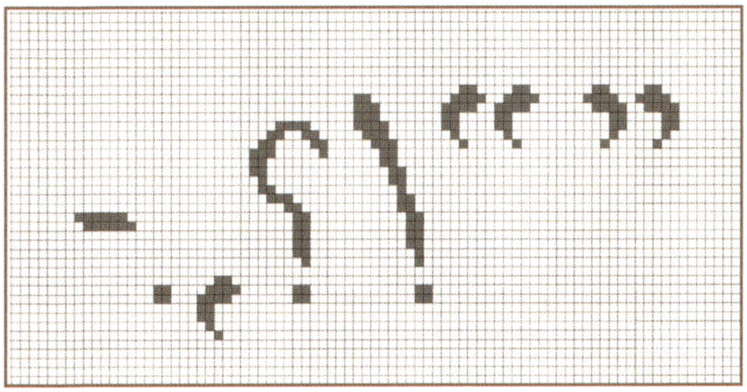

# SELECTED BIBLIOGRAPHY

Beck, Dorothy, and Hazel Chase. *Handwoven Embroidery Weaves*. Woburn, MA, and Sonoma, CA: Privately printed, 1965.

Fairbank, Alfred. *A Book of Scripts*. London: Penguin Books, 1950.

Keasbey, Doramay. *Sheer Delight—Handwoven Transparencies*. Petaluma, CA: Stellar, 1990.

Moorman, Theo. *Weaving as an Art Form—a Personal Statement*. New York: Van Nostrand Reinhold, 1975.

Scanlin, Tommye McClure. "Add Images to Your Weaving with Inlay." *Little Looms*, Spring 2025.

Tate, Lou. *Weaving at the Little Loomhouse*. Louisville: Privately printed, 1940.

Wilson, Jean. *Weaving Is Creative—the Weaver Controlled Weaves*. New York: Van Nostrand Reinhold, 1972.

# INDEX

Photo: Tracey Eller

**Scott Norris** has spent more than three decades dyeing and weaving linen and teaching beginner, intermediate, and advanced weavers. He is a frequent guest lecturer and workshop leader for weaving guilds throughout New England and upstate New York. His love of eighteenth-century book design led to his journey in typographic weaving using the inlay technique.

Scott has received best-in-show honors from the New England Weavers Seminar and has published profiles, essays, and reviews in *American Craft, Ceramics Art and Perception, Ceramics Monthly*, and others. He's also a founding member of Working Weavers Studio Trail, an organization that opens professional weavers' studios to the public.

www.elamswidow.com